The Politics of Class and Class Origin: The Case of the Cultural Revolution

Gordon White

CONTEMPORARY CHINA PAPERS 9

Printed and Published in Australia at
The Australian National University 1976

Printed at:
SOCPAC Printery
The Research Schools of Social Sciences and Pacific Studies, H.C. Coombs Building, ANU

Distributed by:
Contemporary China Centre,
The Australian National University

National Library of Australia Card No. and
ISBN 0 909596 10 7

Gordon White was trained in Chinese politics at Cornell and Stanford Universities. In 1973, he was appointed Lecturer in the Department of Political Science, Faculty of Arts, at The Australian National University in Canberra. The material for this monograph was collected during the author's visits to Hong Kong in 1971-1972 and 1974. He is at present completing a doctoral thesis on the politics of stratification and distribution in contemporary China.

General Editor Frederick C. Teiwes

Other Papers

1 Leong Sow-Theng, *Sino-Soviet Relations: The first phase 1917-1920*. 1971.

2 Robert O'Neill, *Peking-Hanoi Relations in 1970*. 1971.

3 Audrey Donnithorne, *The Budget and the Plan in China: Central-local economic relations*. 1972.

4 Stephen FitzGerald, *Talking with China: The Australian Labor Party visit and Peking's foreign policy*. 1972.

5 Colin Mackerras, *Amateur Theatre in China, 1949-1966*. 1973.

6 Robert Taylor, *Education and University Enrolment Policies in China, 1949-1971*. 1973.

7 Ralph Pettman, *China in Burma's Foreign Policy*. 1973.

8 Leslie W. Chan, *The Taching Oilfield: A Maoist model for economic development*. 1974.

The above numbers may be ordered from:
The Australian National University Press
P.O. Box 4
Canberra, A.C.T., Australia 2600

EDITOR'S FOREWORD

This number of the Contemporary China Papers marks a major change in format and distribution. Previous Papers (listed opposite) have been published and marketed by the Australian National University Press. Cost factors, however, have made this no longer practicable. Therefore, with this study we have converted to a more economical offset process and the Contemporary China Centre itself has undertaken the distribution of the Papers. Keeping costs to a minimum, we are able to sell this Paper by Gordon White for only A$2 (US$3 overseas).

Our next number, *Directory of Central Officials in the People's Republic of China, 1968-1975* by Malcolm Lamb, will be sold for A$4 (US$5 overseas). Lamb's *Directory* provides an extremely useful and in some ways unique research tool for students of contemporary China. According to the foremost expert on the Chinese elite:

> "Lamb's directory will be a real blessing for specialists on China. A directory of Chinese officialdom is always valuable. A cumulative directory providing systematic data on personnel changes over such a substantial period is invaluable." - Donald Klein.

This Paper can now be ordered from the Contemporary China Centre, P.O. Box 4, Canberra, A.C.T., Australia 2600.

We are particularly fortunate to have Gordon White's *The Politics of Class and Class Origin: The Case of the Cultural Revolution* as the initial number under the new format. White's study addresses a central but little examined question of contemporary Chinese politics: how is class conceptualised and precisely how does it affect concrete political processes in today's China - a China where "class struggle" is such a predominant theme. His case study of the Cultural Revolution provides a detailed account of divergent ideological views concerning class, implications of such views for social stratification, conflicting leadership interests in the approach adopted, and factional Red Guard struggles centering on the class issue. The fascinating analysis of the interplay of these factors provides an important advance in our understanding of contemporary Chinese politics.

Frederick C. Teiwes

CONTENTS

ACKNOWLEDGMENTS

I would like to thank Marc Blecher and Fred Teiwes for their helpful comments on various drafts of this monograph, A.T.P. Lee for his help in translating the article "Origin Theory," and Judy McGuigan, Barbara Atkinson and Marcia Milnes for their assistance in preparing the manuscript.

Gordon White
Canberra
October 1975

INTRODUCTION: THE NATURE OF THE PROBLEM

True to the Marxist-Leninist tradition, the Chinese Communists have analysed society and politics primarily in terms of classes and class struggle. They have defined the Chinese revolution as the overthrow of the class order of the "old society" and the creation of a new system where the previously oppressed classes, workers and peasants, exercise social and political hegemony. It is clear, however, that definitions of "class" have varied over time since 1949 and that the view of "class" expounded by Mao Tse-tung differs considerably from the "orthodox" Marxist definition of class rooted in the idea of relationship to the economic means of production. Western scholars have already devoted much attention to Mao Tse-tung's views on the nature of "classes" and "class struggle," notably his redefinition of "class" as an ideological rather than an economic category.[1] This study intends to go beyond the analysis of theoretical innovation by relating changes in the ideological definition of "class" to practical policy issues and to the nature of socio-political interests at various levels of the Chinese political process. These broad themes will be explored in the context of a detailed case study of the conflict over "class" and "class origin" during the Cultural Revolution.

"Class" is a complex phenomenon with manifold implications for contemporary Chinese politics. This study examines "class" in relation to three areas of inquiry: ideological theory, the socio-political structure of Chinese society, and the process of socio-political mobility for China's younger generation. To further this analysis, a case study is made of "class" politics during the Cultural Revolution organised around these three themes.

---

1. For example, see Dennis M. Ray, "Mao and the Classless Society," *Survey*, No.77 (Autumn 1970), pp.30-50; Donald J. Munro, "The Malleability of Man in Chinese Marxism," *The China Quarterly*, No.48 (October-December 1971), pp.609-40; Richard Kraus, "The Evolving Concept of Class in Post-Liberation China" (Ph.D. Dissertation, Columbia University, 1974).

The Ideological Definition of "Class"

It is one of the central tenets of this study that "class" is not merely an abstract ideological category but a term of living political significance, the definition of which has changed in response to the dynamics of modern Chinese politics. It is important, however, to begin by clarifying the different ways in which "class" has been defined by Chinese Communist theorists, notably Mao Tse-tung. There have been two dominant meanings attributed to "class" in post-Liberation Chinese politics which I have chosen to refer to as the "old" and the "new" definitions of class.

(*i*) "Old" Classes or Class *Ch'eng-fen*

In the pre-Liberation and immediate post-Liberation period, the CCP leadership defined class primarily in socio-economic terms. In 1950, the Party embarked on a nation-wide programme which classified Chinese citizens according to their class "composition" or "*ch'eng-fen*" (hereafter referred to as "class *ch'eng-fen*" or simply "*ch'eng-fen*"). Detailed regulations were issued in 1950 to guide the process of class demarcation in rural areas and the resulting categorisation provided the social and political basis for the programme of agrarian revolution which led through land reform to collectivisation.[2] Although urban class structure was also demarcated in the 1950's, the process seems to have been more piecemeal, informal and unsystematic, with correspondingly more scope for ambiguity in the years to follow.

According to the regulations issued in 1950, a person's *ch'eng-fen* was assigned according to the source of his economic support in the three years preceding 1949. The practical

---

2. "Decisions concerning the Differentiation of Class Status in the Countryside," adopted by the Government Administration Council for the Central People's Government on August 4, 1950, in a supplement to *People's China*, Vol.II, No.8, October 16, 1950, pp.3-16. For a Chinese text, see *Tsen-yang fen-hsi nung-ts'un chieh-chi* [How to Analyse Rural Classes] (Peking: Jen-min ch'u-pan-she, 1966).
   For a contemporary discussion of the Decisions, see Liao Lu-yen, "Rural class status and land reform," *People's China* (supplement), Vol.II, No.8, October 16, 1950, pp.17-20.

reference of *ch'eng-fen* extended beyond broad class categories (*chieh-chi*) such as "workers," "capitalists" or "landlords." It was used to differentiate strata within classes (such as "poor peasants"), amorphous economic strata (such as urban "poor people") and relatively narrow occupational groups (such as "free professionals," "employees," "revolutionary cadres" and "revolutionary soldiers"). Given this wide range of reference, it is somewhat of a misnomer to equate *ch'eng-fen* with *class* status in the strict sense. Thus the Chinese term "class *ch'eng-fen*" carries this ambiguity within it.

According to the documents of August 1950, class *ch'eng-fen* was to be distinguished from "class origin" (*chieh-chi ch'u-shen*) or "family origin" (*chia-t'ing ch'u-shen*) (the meanings of these two latter terms being virtually identical):

> The family origin of children and young students: All children and young students at school under the age of 18 should not in general have a class *ch'eng-fen* assigned to them. Exception is made for those who are already head of a family at the time of land reform. In such cases, their class *ch'eng-fen* should be determined.[3]

Thus the "class origin" of a young person was to depend on the class *ch'eng-fen* of his parents (in practical terms, the class *ch'eng-fen* of his "family head," usually his father).

In spite of these initial formal definitions which distinguished class "composition" (*ch'eng-fen*) from class or family "origin" (*ch'u-shen*), throughout the following two decades there has been a great deal of confusion among both cadres and populace over the precise use of the two terms. The distinction between them has been blurred in practice. The term "family *ch'eng-fen*" (*chia-t'ing ch'eng-fen*), for example, has been used synonymously with "family origin" (*chia-t'ing ch'u-shen*). As a result, a middle school student in the 1960's who was, say, from a worker's family, would often describe himself loosely as having worker *ch'eng-fen* instead of using the more precise term *ch'u-shen* or "origin." Popular confusion over these terms found recurring expression in the Chinese

---

3. "Decisions concerning Differentiation," Section III, Article 9.

press, particularly in the early and mid-1960's,[4] and Red Guard polemics on the class theme during the Cultural Revolution concentrated a great deal, as we shall see in the case study, on the conceptual ambiguity between "*ch'eng-fen*" and "origin."[5]

(*ii*) "New" Classes: the Political-Ideological Notion of Class

When the transformation of Chinese socio-economic structure had been basically completed by 1956, the Chinese leadership came to the conclusion that the "old" socio-economic class categories had lost most of their political force.[6] With the events of the late 1950's and early 1960's, however, Mao Tse-tung himself, accompanied by a minority segment of the Party, reacted to a series of threatening political events and social trends by moving towards the elaboration of a new definition of "class" in the context of a "new class struggle" at the political and ideological levels.[7] The new analysis focused on the development of a new class system emerging partly from attitudinal "hangovers" from the old society and partly from the structure of the new socialist society with its occupational, economic and political differentials which provided the "social basis" for a new system of class inequalities. This vision crystallised in Mao's speech to the Tenth Plenum of the Eighth

---

4. For example, "One ought to define and view correctly the family origin and class *ch'eng-fen* of youth and children," *Chung-kuo Ch'ing-nien* [China Youth] (hereafter *CKCN*), No.13, July 1, 1962, p.24; "On what basis is 'family background' determined? Can it be changed?" *Chung-kuo Ch'ing-nien Pao* [China Youth Daily] (hereafter *CKCNP*), December 27, 1962, in *Survey of China Mainland Press* (hereafter *SCMP*) No.2896, pp.4-5.
5. For a discussion of the impact of class and other labels on political conflict during the initial stages of the Cultural Revolution, see Gordon A. Bennett, "Political Labels and Popular Tension," *Current Scene*, February 26, 1969, pp.1-15.
6. For an authoritative statement of the apparent consensus view at the time, see Liu Shao-ch'i, "The Political Report of the Central Committee of the CPC to the Eighth National Congress of the Party," September 15, 1956, in *Eighth National Congress of the Communist Party of China* (Peking: Foreign Languages Press, 1956), Vol.I, pp.15-111.
7. This is discussed most comprehensively in Kraus, "The Evolving Concept of Class," pp.138-215.

Central Committee of the Party in 1962 and was elaborated further by the Chairman over the succeeding years.[8] The distinguishing criterion of a person's status in this new class order rested on his political behaviour (*piao-hsien*) and attitudes (*szu-hsiang*). According to the new theory, there was no *necessary* connection between a person's objective class *ch'eng-fen* or class origin on the one hand and his or her class standing in the attitudinal-behavioural sense on the other. Thus it was quite possible for industrial workers to be infected by "bourgeois ideology" and for high-ranking Party cadres to degenerate into "new bourgeois elements." In theory, moreover, it was quite possible for, say, the son of a capitalist or a landlord to become "proletarianised" given the right mix of personal determination and external encouragement.

During the 1960's, therefore, there were two institutionalised definitions of "class" in China. The old socio-economically based *ch'eng-fen* categories retained much of their original political force, *being overlaid rather than replaced* by the new metamorphosis of class. Behind this theoretical ambiguity, one can see an intersection of different historical stages of modern Chinese revolutionary politics: the continued influence of the "old" class struggle led by the CCP against "counter-revolutionary" classes and groups of pre-1949 society and the beginning of a perceived new stage of political development when the contradictions within the new socialist society became the focus of ideological debate and political conflict. These two models of socio-political conflict coexisted in a complex process of mutual interplay under the general ideological rubric of the "continuing revolution."

This basic ambiguity was further complicated by three other factors: first, the original economically based concept of class *ch'eng-fen* expanded its range of reference to include groups defined in *political* terms and differentiated by political labels or *mao-tzu* (lit. "hats"). Thus, the "worst"

---

8. Kraus provides a detailed analysis of Mao's statements on the issue, both public and private, during the 1960's in Chapter 3, *ibid*.

ch'eng-fen in China in the 1960's were those of the "five elements" (*wu lei fen-tzu*), namely "landlords, rich peasants, counter-revolutionaries, bad elements and rightists." Of these five categories, only two were socio-economic class categories ("landlord" and "rich peasant"), while two were political ("counter-revolutionary" and "rightist") and one judicial ("bad element").[9] Second, the new political-ideological definition of class was hard to operationalise in everyday political practice. Although certain criteria were laid down by Mao himself, they remained fuzzy and subject to the ideological predispositions and political affiliations of cadres who had the authority to make concrete definitions at each level. When centres of authority proliferated, moreover, as they did during the Cultural Revolution, operational criteria for assigning people to distinct class categories also proliferated, further complicating the process of class definition. Third, divergent theoretical definitions of class have had differential political impact on, and meaning for, different sections of the leadership and the general population. As a result, theoretical class categories became enmeshed with sectional political and social interests and, in the Cultural Revolution, they functioned as ideological banners in a factionalised political process. The following case study will illustrate this interplay of ideology and interest, theory and practice, at work during the early stages of the Cultural Revolution.

The Socio-Political Structure of Chinese Society in the Early and Mid-1960's

Passing from ideological theory to socio-political reality, the structure of Chinese "society" in the 1960's contained elements of both "old" and "new" class systems. Original *ch'eng-fen* categories, increasingly detached from their original economic references, were fused with political labels, invidious or honorific, to function as marks of "good" or "bad" political

9. For the legal aspects of these labels, see Jerome A. Cohen, *The Criminal Process in the People's Republic of China 1949-1963: An Introduction* (Cambridge, Mass.: Harvard University Press, 1968).

status. Remnants of the "old" domestic class enemies were linked both with their counterparts in Taiwan and to the continuing international class structure dominated by imperialists and reactionaries. The official media, particularly after 1962, extolled the virtues of the revolutionary classes and warned the population of the iniquitous potential of "landlords" and other "class enemies." Official policies on educational, occupational and political recruitment stressed the need to favour those groups with "better" *ch'eng-fen* and their offspring. Thus both *ch'eng-fen* and family origin became bases for a hierarchical differentiation of political status with significant implications for the individual's life chances in the new society. In this sense, the "old" class structure was stood on its head and incorporated as an important element of stratification in the new society.

But the 1960's also brought an increasing awareness among significant sections of the Party membership and general population of the emergence of new forms of inequality which grew out of the structure of the socialist system established in 1956 and afterwards. There were trends towards the development of two elite groups. First, the institutionalised inequalities of power deriving from the logic of the vanguard Party were leading to the formation of a power elite with its own sense of superior solidarity, life-style and special economic and social privileges which were increasingly transmitted to the next generation. Second, meritocratic educational recruitment and conciliatory policies towards the intelligentsia were leading to the development of a new social elite composed of university-trained specialists and professionals. In general terms, the unevenness of the economic structure (notably the urban-rural gap), occupational stratification and the impact of certain of the Party's key economic and social policies (notably a policy of differentiated wages and the campaign to send urban youth to the countryside) led to the formation of groups or strata which perceived themselves to be relatively disadvantaged: urban "intellectual youth" sent to the countryside to become peasants; unskilled urban workers; temporary or contract workers; students in low-quality urban schools; and unemployed urban "street youth" (or "social youth"). It was these inequalities and the trend towards the inter-generational transmission of privilege and underprivilege that stimulated and gave substance to radical warnings about the emergence of a "new" class system.

Given the emergence in the 1960's of this new system of inequalities, both "objective" and subjectively defined, competition for access to higher-valued roles became fierce and heavily concentrated on mobility within the educational system and, if a "political career" were aspired to, on access to the Communist Youth League and the Party. It is in this area of social and political mobility that the link between the "old" class structure and the new system of socio-economic stratification became most apparent. Given the fact that, to varying degrees at different times and within different social sectors, a person's *ch'eng-fen* or class origin had some influence in facilitating or hampering his access to opportunity, these "old" class factors became an important issue in the minds of young people going through China's high schools in the early and mid-1960's. This brings us to our third area of inquiry and the major topic of the case study, the impact of class categories on the attitudes and behaviour of Chinese youth in the new socialist society of the 1960's.

Educated Urban Youth and the Politics of Mobility

In the early and mid-1960's, the future prospects of urban Chinese youth, in terms of educational, occupational and political mobility, depended on three criteria: skill or academic competence measured by educational performance, political behaviour (*cheng-chih piao-hsien*), and class or family origin. The relative salience of these criteria varied according to the period and the specific context of the individual case (for example, political behaviour and class origin were more important for allocation to a military academy than, say, to a college of fine arts). The three criteria are manifestations, in the field of educational, occupational and political allocation of Chinese youth, of three of the basic political priorities of the Chinese Communist Party (CCP): (a) the criterion of skill and academic competence reflects the priority attached to economic modernisation and technological development; (b) the criterion of political behaviour reflects the priority placed on attitudinal transformation, the inculcation of the proletarian values and behaviour of the new "class" order; (c) the criterion of family origin reflects the redistributive priorities implicit in the idea of the "class line" (*chieh-chi lu-hsien*). In this aspect, the "class line" is a concept of revolutionary egalitarianism designed to redistribute social, economic and political opportunity in favour of the labouring classes and their offspring and to restrict or remove the privileges of previous elites in a wide range of policy areas: in political recruitment, military conscription, educational opportunity and job placement. In educational policy, for example, the Party saw the school system from the outset as an instrument for transforming the pre-revolutionary class system. Thus in his report to the First National Educational Work Conference in May 1950 the then Vice Minister of Education, Ch'ien Chün-jui, described the "class line" in education as follows:

> In the whole nation, 80 percent of the population is composed of workers, peasants and broad masses, and their sons and daughters are basically still shut outside the doors of the schools. To resolutely change these conditions, to cause education to be truly a democratic education, to serve truly the cause of raising high the cultural and political level of the workers and peasants, and to cause the various classes of schools to open their doors for the sons and daughters of the workers, peasants and broad masses is something that can no longer be postponed.[10]

Although the impact of the "class line" in education and other policy sectors has varied over time, it has exerted a continuing influence on the life chances of Chinese youth by

---

10. Ch'ien Chün-jui, "General Policy of Present Educational Construction," May 1950, in John N. Hawkins, trans., *Educational Theory in the People's Republic of China: The Report of Ch'ien Chün-jui*, Asian Studies at Hawaii, No.6, Asian Studies Program, University of Hawaii, 1971, p.72.

attempting to give preferential treatment to youth of "good" class origins.[11]

Of these three criteria for evaluating Chinese youth, the relationship between the skill-achievement criterion on the one hand and the two political criteria on the other has been discussed *in extenso* by Western scholars - this is one crucial aspect of the familiar "red-expert" problem.[12] The main focus in this study, however, is on the relationship between the latter two political criteria. How has the Party reconciled the universalistic, achievement-oriented criterion of "political behaviour," reflecting the ideological definition of "class" as a question of attitudes and behaviour, with the selective, ascriptive criterion of class origin, reflecting the redistributive priorities of the socio-economically rooted "class line?"

In the 1960's, Party leaders attempted to relate the two political criteria through what came to be known as the "*class policy*" (*chieh-chi cheng-ts'e*). The policy rested on three ideas, capsulised in the following terse instructions to cadres: "pay attention to *ch'eng-fen* [or origin], but don't pay exclusive attention to *ch'eng-fen* [or origin]; put the major stress on [political] behaviour."[13] In other words, the

---

11. For a detailed analysis of the impact of the class line on university recruitment policies, see Robert Taylor, *Education and University Enrolment Policies in China, 1949-1971* (Canberra: Australian National University Press, 1973).
12. For example, see Richard Baum, "'Red and Expert': The Politico-Ideological Foundations of China's Great Leap Forward," *Asian Survey*, September 1964, pp.1048-57; Dennis Ray, "Red and Expert in China's Cultural Revolution," *Pacific Affairs*, Spring 1970, pp.22-33; Martin K. Whyte, "'Red vs. Expert': Peking's Changing Policy," *Problems of Communism*, November-December 1972, pp.18-27.
13. Although these ideas underlay the official attitude to the issue from at least 1961 onwards, the "class policy" was not codified systematically and identified as such until 1965, the political impetus being provided by the Second Plenum of the YCL Central Committee in March-April of that year. For a comprehensive exposition of the "class policy" in this period, see "Stressing behaviour is the Party's class policy," *CKCN*, No.18, September 16, 1965, pp.2-5.

official "class policy" was based on the assumption that, although class origin should be accorded some independent significance in evaluating and advancing a young person politically, the primary emphasis should be on his political behaviour which was held to have no necessarily predictable relationship with family origin. Behaviour being equal, however, the youth of "better" class origin would enjoy an advantage over a youth of "worse" origin. There was also an implicit assumption that family origin exerted an important influence over political behaviour. Thus, youth of good origins were assumed to have a political advantage owing to the beneficial "class stamp" (*chieh-chi lo-yin*) imprinted by their families. But such youth were warned not to assume that their good class origins automatically made them "red" politically: this was the mistake of "natural redness" (*tzu-lai-hung*).[14] On the other hand, the "class policy" recognised that youths from "exploiting class" origins would find it more difficult to reach acceptable levels of political consciousness and behaviour because of the deleterious influence of their families. If they were prepared, however, to "turn their backs on their families" (*pei-p'an chia-t'ing*) by "drawing a clear [ideological] dividing line" (*hua-ch'ing chieh-hsien*), then they too could join the "class ranks" of the proletariat.[15]

In the years leading up to the Cultural Revolution, attitudes on the issue of class origin were clouded by several kinds of ambiguity. These stemmed ultimately from the attempt to combine two disparate political principles, class origin and political behaviour. In spite of the clear priority attached to the behavioural criterion, there was much scope left for

---

14. For a critique of "natural redness," see Sun Yi-ch'ing, "Lay down the load; advance with light equipment," *CKCNP*, November 17, 1964, in *SCMP* No.3349, pp.1-6.
15. One of the models chosen to illustrate this process was Sun Yün-chieh, a girl from a rich peasant family. For her story, see Sun Yün-chieh, "I rebel against the exploiting class and join the Communist Party," *CKCN*, No.16, August 16, 1965, pp.19-21. The same issue of *CKCN* published an editorial on her case: "Embark upon a revolutionary road like Sun Yün-chieh," *op.cit.*, p.18, in *Survey of China Mainland Magazines* (hereafter *SCMM*), No.494, pp.19-20.

confusion and variation in the process of translating this ranking into practice. In fact, the Central leadership varied the relative weight attached to the two standards at different periods during the early and mid-1960's, from a "right" tendency to neglect the influence of class origin to a "left" tendency to regard it as decisively important - the latter being referred to as the "theory of only [stressing class] *ch'eng-fen* (or class origin)" (*wei ch'eng-fen-lun* or *wei ch'u-shen-lun*).

Thus, in the "liberalisation" atmosphere of 1960-61, the class criterion was muted, particularly in the field of educational recruitment. This is noticeable, for example, in Ch'en Yi's famous speech to Peking college graduates in August 1961. Criticising "those who have one-sidedly put stress on the family origin" of young students from "exploiting class" backgrounds, Ch'en emphasised that a youth could not choose what family he or she was born into and that, in these changed times, an unfavourable class origin did not prevent young people from becoming revolutionaries. The key factors, he continued, were the individual's own aspirations and the nature of his educational environment:

> Now it is already twelve years after liberation... If a youth from an exploiting class family origin is 22 years old today, he was 10 in the year of liberation, a very young age. It must be said that the influence of his exploiting class family on him will be relatively small. Today's students are all children of our Party, our people and our nation. If they make an effort themselves and if we educate them properly as well, then they can all become our good cadres. If they do not make a personal effort and if we educate them badly, even if they are children of workers and peasants or cadres' children, they can also change for the worse. We should treat them as our own children when we educate them and should not draw an uncrossable line between worker-peasant youth and youth of exploiting class family origin.[16]

---

16. Ch'en Yi, "Speech to students about to graduate from Peking's institutions of higher education," *CKCN*, No.17, September 1, 1961, p.4.

During 1963 and 1964, however, the emphasis on family origin was strengthened, particularly in the areas of Youth League and general leadership recruitment.[17] For example, a *People's Daily* editorial in August 1964 stated that the primary emphasis in the recruitment of a new "leadership nucleus" should be laid on young people from good class backgrounds:

> Attention must be paid to making sure that people of good class and family origin, who have been tempered for a long period through class struggle, account for the greatest majority of the nucleus of the leadership of the revolutionary ranks of the proletariat. This is the class basis for guaranteeing that the revolutionary ranks and nucleus of the leadership will never change colour.[18]

In 1965, however, there was a reorientation of the "class policy" for recruitment to the Youth League. Statements by key Party leaders, notably P'eng Chen in his speech to the Second Session of the Fourth Congress of the All-China Federation of Democratic Youth in early 1965, emphasised the need to give priority to the behavioural criterion in the political evaluation of youth.[19] The Second Plenum of the Ninth Youth League Central Committee, which met in March-April 1965, gave priority to a relaxation of the criterion of class origin in League recruitment and to the role of the League in "uniting with the broad masses of youth," including those whose origins were not good.[20] This change in emphasis was to have significant impact on events during the early stages of the Cultural Revolution for two reasons: first, because in the

---

17. For example, see Chang Yüan-chin, "Recruit new League members according to plan," *CKCNP*, November 7, 1963, in *SCMP* No.3115, p.4.
18. "Full text of the *People's Daily* editorial on cultivation of successors to the proletarian revolutionary cause," New China News Agency (hereafter NCNA), August 3, 1964, in *SCMP* No.3274, pp.4-5.
19. For a discussion of the implications of P'eng's report, see "Correctly deal with class origins, resolutely tread the road of revolutionisation - some educated youth in the Sian area hold an informal meeting to talk about what they have learnt from Comrade P'eng Chen's report," *Kuang-ming Jih-pao* [Kuang-ming Daily] (hereafter *KMJP*), April 5, 1965, in *SCMP* No.3441.
20. For example, see Kao Tse-hung, "Get the overwhelming majority of youth united," *CKCN*, No.10, May 16, 1965, in *SCMM* No.479, pp.13-16.

campaign against P'eng Chen in mid-1966, this "rightist" redefinition of the "class policy" was cited as evidence of his "revisionism" and, second, because it clearly encountered much resistance and scepticism among both youth and cadres, feelings which were to find political expression in the summer of 1966.[21]

Given such fluctuations in the official interpretation of "class policy" and given its inherent ambiguity, it is not surprising that basic level cadres encountered difficulties in implementation. The main source of ideological guidance was Mao Tse-tung but, in both public and private utterances, the Chairman was ambiguous on the subject. The ideological-behavioural definition of class clearly dominated his thoughts in the early and mid-1960's, finding its clearest expression in his five standards for judging "revolutionary successors" published in July 1964. It is clear, however, that he was not willing to sever completely the umbilical relationship between class as an objective and a subjective phenomenon.[22] Mao's ambiguity thus left scope for varying interpretations and, particularly if the whole corpus of his published works were used as reference and not merely contemporary statements, the field for divergent interpretations was even wider.

Thus cadre "deviations" in the implementation of "class policy" were common in the years before the Cultural Revolution. Leaving temporal fluctuations in policy aside for a moment, there were structural factors which fostered both "right" deviations (i.e. neglect of class origin) and "left" deviations (i.e. excessive stress on class origin, often called "only origin theory"). In the competitive, quality-oriented

---

21. This scepticism is evident in an artificial discussion between "Little Chang" and "Old Wang," published in *CKCN*: Hsiang Nung, "The class policy which attaches importance to behaviour must be implemented," *CKCN*, No.17, September 1, 1965, in *SCMM* No.495, pp.35-38.
22. For a detailed discussion of this topic, see Kraus, "The Evolving Concept of Class," Chapter 3. For Mao's five standards, see *On Krushchev's Phoney Communism and its Historical Lessons for the World* (July 14, 1964) (Peking: Foreign Languages Press, 1964), pp.73-74.

environment of China's schools in the first half of the 1960's, there was implicit pressure to minimise the constraints imposed by the class origin criterion on the process of selection of the academically fittest. On the other hand, there were contrary pressures, particularly strong with regard to political recruitment but not negligible in educational and occupational recruitment, which stemmed from the clash between the behavioural emphasis of the "class policy" and the fact that, particularly from 1963 to 1966, China's general political environment was heavily impregnated with "old" class themes. Given the constant warnings about the continued influences of former "class enemies," the constant stress on the inherent virtues of the labouring classes, the considerable attention paid to "old" class categories during the Socialist Education Movement and the continuing pressure on cadres to keep their social and political relationships free from "class taint," it is not surprising that many cadres "preferred 'left' to 'right'" by stressing origin over behaviour in their implementation of "class policy." This tendency towards "only origin theory" in making concrete choices offered cadres two advantages: first, in judging political virtue and reliability family origin was much easier to use than the criterion of behaviour which was difficult to monitor and assess. Second, an overemphasis on family origin involved less potential risk than an overemphasis on behaviour. If the cadre were faulted by his superiors for paying too much attention to class and neglecting political performance, his mistakes could well be interpreted as a well-intentioned but over-enthusiastic attempt to achieve legitimate long-term aims and thus would bring no serious political repercussions. If the cadre erred in the other direction, however, he ran the risk of being criticised for "lacking a firm class stand" which carried far more serious political implications. As the events of the Cultural Revolution showed, such apprehensions were not without foundation.

To summarise, it is clear that in the minds of urban educated youth in the early and mid-1960's the meaning of "class" was ambiguous. The different meanings of "class," moreover, had crucial implications for the ability of urban youth to realise their aspirations in life. Fluctuations in the relative emphasis on political performance and family origin within the official "class policy" had varying impact on different sectors of educated youth. Given the complexities stemming from ideological ambiguity, policy fluctuation and variations in policy implementation, it is not surprising to find that, on the eve of the Cultural Revolution, a wide range of discontents had developed among diverse sections of urban youth. Judging from the Chinese press and interview data, we can discern four groups. (*i*) The children of "revolutionary cadres" and "revolutionary armymen": This group should be distinguished from the sons and daughters of ordinary cadres. The two terms imply that the parents concerned were already active in the revolutionary cause before 1949. Thus they would, by and large, have reached relatively high-ranking positions in the civilian and military bureaucracies by the 1960's. Their children were in a relatively privileged position: in the political atmosphere of the early and mid-1960's, their family origin was considered to be "best," so they benefited most from the "class line" in socio-political recruitment. The identity of their parents exerted informal, implicit pressures on teachers and basic-level administrators which led to special treatment and made direct parental intervention on their behalf the exception rather than the rule. Their elite position was reinforced by special schools which recruited only the sons and daughters of cadres.[23] Their relatively favourable family environment, moreover, tended to encourage academic achievement and, more importantly, provided a sense of political savoir faire and self-confidence which guaranteed a high rate of access to the Young Communist League and a high evaluation for "reliable" and "active" political behaviour. Although relatively well placed in terms of all the three criteria used to evaluate youth, they

---

23. For a discussion of this problem, see John Gardner, "Educated Youth and Urban-Rural Inequalities," in John W. Lewis, ed., *The City in Communist China* (Stanford, Calif.: Stanford University Press, 1971), pp.256-57.

favoured the two political criteria, a position which was consonant with both their political beliefs and their social interests. They resented, on both ideological and interest grounds, any overstress on academic competence which favoured youth from intelligentsia and "exploiting class" backgrounds. To them, this was politically immoral, since it contravened the "class line," and personally threatening insofar as it reduced their own access to desirable opportunity. (*ii*) Worker-peasant youth: Although they shared the advantage of "good" family origin with the first category, this group had less advantages in the competition for access to social opportunity. They too tended to favour the two political criteria of class origin and behaviour over the academic criterion but they lacked the political skills and advantages of "revolutionary cadre" children. Particularly in the case of poor and lower-middle peasant children, moreover, they lacked a family environment conducive to academic achievement and thus fared poorly on the academic criterion. There was a tendency, therefore, for them to resent "clever" youth, particularly those of urban intelligentsia origin. Their resentment was tempered somewhat, however, by the apparent fact that, as a group, they had somewhat lower horizons than youths in the first and third categories. (*iii*) Youth from "middling" (*chung-teng*) class origins: This group was in an ambiguous but not altogether unfavourable position. Though they were impeded to some extent by their class origin, they were often able, particularly those from intellectual or professional families, to recoup their impaired political status through positive political behaviour and high levels of academic achievement. Although they tended to accept the validity of the behavioural criterion, they resented the privileges attaching to good family origin and opposed an overemphasis on political criteria *vis a vis* academic achievement. (*iv*) Youth of "exploiting class" background: While they had benefited from the reduced impact of both political criteria during 1960 and 1961, this group increasingly lost ground as the "class line" was intensified after 1962. They were doubly disadvantaged. First, the criterion of "class origin" made their own background a heavy "burden" blocking social advancement and creating pessimism and passivity. Second, their attempts to "demand progress" (*yao-ch'iu chin-pu*) through positive behaviour were often stifled by the common tendency of basic-level cadres to ignore the salvational aspect of the "class policy" and to regard progressive behaviour on the part of "exploiting class" youth as either phoney or unimportant. Thus, though many such youth accepted the legitimacy of the behavioural criterion, they were frustrated by its implementation. In general, they opposed the attention paid to class origin in socio-political recruitment and resented the rights and privileges which it gave to their fellow students from good origins.

Thus, on the eve of the Cultural Revolution, Chinese urban youth had formed different constellations of interests and attitudes in relation to the meaning of "class" terms and the impact of class-related policies. The differential impact of the "class policy" on the competition for advancement led to tension which accumulated at key transitional points in the social process: application for League or Party membership, recruitment to cadre positions (for example, League or school class cadres), access to senior middle schools or colleges, and allocation to different types of employment after school or college. At the ideological level, the principle of redistributive revolutionary egalitarianism reflected in the "class line" and "class policy" had gained uneven acceptance among Chinese youth, competing in their minds with other egalitarian principles affirming equality of opportunity regardless of class origin (based on either academic attainment or political behaviour or both). The following case study shows how these divisions and disagreements came to express themselves in the fluid political process which emerged in China during the Cultural Revolution.

THE CASE STUDY: THE POLITICS OF CLASS AND CLASS ORIGIN IN THE CULTURAL REVOLUTION

This case study examines how the diverse ideological definitions, political attitudes and social interests coexisting in China in the early 1960's were activated into a complex process of political interplay during the period from mid-1966 to mid-1967. The Cultural Revolution brought a sharp change in political context which widened the scope of ideological debate, vastly increased the number of active participants in the political process and allowed, albeit in disguised form, the articulation of diverse sectional interests.[24] In this changed environment, the accumulated ideological ambiguities, submerged social tensions and informal political solidarities which had developed in response to the issue of "class" were expressed overtly in organised and often programmatic form. Focusing on the dispute between rival Red Guard groups over the political significance of the class origin of a young person in the new society, this study demonstrates how the official pre-Cultural Revolution "class policy" came under attack on both flanks from two variant conceptions of the "class policy," both apparently generated at the grass roots level, which crystallised the fundamental differences between "old" and "new" class definitions in political form. Differences over the "class policy" at the mass level were closely linked to the ideological and political struggle within the Party leadership.

At the leadership level, the Cultural Revolution following Mao's personal initiative first attacked key officials who, among other things, were accused of favouring "old" exploiting classes on redistributive issues. Soon, however, these "old" redistributive issues became overlaid by

---

24. For a useful analysis of the role of occupational differentiation in structuring mass politics during the Cultural Revolution, see Michel Oksenberg, "Occupational groups in Chinese society and the Cultural Revolution," in M. Oksenberg et al., *The Cultural Revolution: 1967 in Review*, Michigan Papers in Chinese Studies, No.2, 1968, pp.1-39.

a new conflict involving both the power positions of individual leaders of "good" class *ch'eng-fen* and critiques of the redistribution these leaders as a group had brought about in their own favour. Thus, by mid-summer 1966, a struggle developed between so-called "revisionist" Party cadres who defined "class," in the context of the Cultural Revolution, in terms of *ch'eng-fen* categories and their "Maoist" or "radical" opponents who used "new" class definitions to label these same cadres as members of a "privileged stratum" of "new bourgeois elements" who were to be the proper targets of the movement. At the level of educated urban youth, a struggle developed between youth from the "good" classes who defined class in terms of the "old" categories and a "rebel" opposition of motley class origins who demanded that the official "class policy" be changed to bring it into line with the behavioural definition of "class." Since the Cultural Revolution involved a dynamic interplay between leader and masses, the conflict and debate over "class" issues at each level interpenetrated to form a multi-faceted and multi-level political process in which the factors of ideology, policy, power and interest became fused. Since no "side" in the debate was able to gain outright victory, the Cultural Revolution did not provide basic solutions to these issues with the result that they continued to be sources of ambiguity and tension in the post-Cultural Revolution era.

This case study is based primarily on articles in Red Guard and Revolutionary Rebel tabloids with some supplementary information from interviews in Hong Kong. Since most of the materials available on the issue of class origin are from Peking and Canton, this study will mainly focus on the situation in those two cities. Since both of those cities are, in different ways, *sui generis*, the conclusions of the study must be viewed with this qualification in mind.

The material is presented chronologically and mainly covers the period from June 1966 to April 1967, with a closing summary of trends in the later stages of the Cultural Revolution and its aftermath. The <u>first stage</u>, from June to mid-August 1966, brought a backlash against attempts to liberalise the "class line" in educational and political recruitment in the preceding two years. "Old" definitions of class were re-emphasised in the official media and Party committees singled out "old" class enemies for attack. As the political thrust of the Cultural Revolution was radicalised during July and August, however, the stress on "old" class categories came to be seen by radical "Maoist" leaders as a conservative ploy used by threatened Party leaders to divert the "spearhead" of the movement. At the level of Red Guard organisations, a similar process took place as the initial emphasis on extending the privileges of worker-peasant youth developed into an extreme version of the "class policy" (called either "only origin theory" or "blood pedigree theory") which claimed that class origin was the main way to assess the revolutionary qualities of youth. This came to be seen by "rebel" Red Guards as a device to avoid the real issues of the Cultural Revolution, to protect the privileges enjoyed by a minority of young people, notably the sons and daughters of high-ranking cadres, and to restrict membership in the new Red Guard organisations.

The second stage, from late August to the end of December 1966, was one of struggle between "conservative" and "rebel" forces. The "new" political analysis of class gained ground as radical leaders in Peking set their sights on "capitalist roaders" within the Party hierarchy. New "rebel" Red Guard groups sprang up to challenge the early organisations, dubbing them "conservatives," because of their close links with the previous authority structure. "Blood pedigree theory" came under heavy attack and the criteria for admission to Red Guard organisations were liberalised and, by the end of 1966, the "rebels" had seized the political initiative. A third stage began in early January when the Peking leadership officially branded "blood pedigree theory" as heterodox. The political predominance of the "rebel" faction in the first two months of 1967 was accompanied by the emergence of an ideological challenge to "blood pedigree theory," known as "origin theory," which argued that the factor of class origin was of negligible significance in evaluating the revolutionary qualities of youth and that the sole criterion should be political behaviour. From February to April 1967, there was a heated debate over the validity of "origin theory" between rival Red Guard tabloids.

Articles on the subject petered out in the Red Guard press in the latter half of 1967 and the Red Guard press itself was eclipsed in 1968. In the later phases of the movement and during its aftermath, the Peking leadership reiterated the ambiguous pre-Cultural Revolution "class policy" as orthodoxy. At the ideological level, both "old" and "new" definitions of "class" were maintained in uneasy juxtaposition, testifying to the issues left unresolved by the Cultural Revolution and reflecting the fundamental ambiguities and tensions which have characterised the Chinese political process in the aftermath of the Cultural Revolution.

Phase 1 - June-August 1966: "Conservative" Class Analysis and the Rise of "Blood Pedigree Theory"

In the first stage, the Cultural Revolution was seen as an expression of "class struggle" but the latter was conceptualised primarily in terms of "old" class categories. Criticism tended to be directed against "old" class enemies, notably the "five elements" and "bourgeois intellectuals." Though a small number of cadres within the Party were brought to task, this rectification was also phrased in terms of the "old" class system: P'eng Chen and others were criticised for discriminating against youth of good class origins in education and in recruitment to the Young Communist League (YCL). In short, although other issues (such as disguised criticism of Mao in the early 1960's) were involved and different segments of the Party leadership clearly had divergent expectations concerning the Cultural Revolution, initially the campaign appeared to combine a relatively limited intra-Party rectification with somewhat ritualised attacks on pre-existing class enemies and deviant intellectuals.[25] As such, there was no implicit threat to the Party hierarchy.

The movement began with an offensive against P'eng Chen, First Secretary of the Peking City Party Committee and one of the most powerful figures on the central Party Politburo and Secretariat. The campaign in each educational institution was managed by Party committees who defined "class enemies" primarily in terms of bad *ch'eng-fen* or class origin, thus directing the major focus of the attack on politically vulnerable targets outside the Party.[26] In middle schools, for example, this meant that staff members of bad class *ch'eng-fen* or origin or with "complex political histories" bore the brunt of organised mass criticism, being labelled "rightists," "representatives of the black gang," "freaks and monsters" or "bourgeois authorities."

In June, the class theme was linked specifically to the proposed change in college admission procedures, a decision announced in a notice issued by the CCP Central Committee and the State Council on June 13 and reinforced by a *People's*

---

25. For example, see Gordon A. Bennett and Ronald N. Montaperto, *Red Guard: The Political Biography of Dai Hsiao-ai* (New York, N.Y.: Anchor Books, 1972), pp.36-40; Ronald N. Montaperto, "From Revolutionary Successors to Revolutionaries: Chinese Students in the Early Stages of the Cultural Revolution," in Robert A. Scalapino, ed., *Elites in the People's Republic of China* (Seattle, Wash.: University of Washington Press, 1972), pp.583-84.
26. Articles attacking the national intellectual targets usually contained sections which cast aspersions on the malevolent influence of their class background. For example, see Ch'i Li and Meng Chin, "Unveiling the true counter-revolutionary face of Wu Han - information from an investigation at Wutien Commune, home of Wu Han in Iwu county," *Jen-min Jih-pao* [People's Daily] (hereafter *JMJP*), May 20, 1966, in *SCMP* No.3718, pp.1-5, which delivers a scathing attack on Wu Han's grandfather, father and mother.

Daily editorial on June 18.[27] This announcement was followed by a spate of articles denouncing the previous educational system as "revisionist" and accusing the previous Peking City Party Committee under P'eng Chen of seriously distorting the "class line." "Entrenched bourgeois academic authorities" in educational institutions, it was claimed, had shown their class nature by conspiring with these "agents of the bourgeoisie" in the Party to discriminate against youth from worker-peasant, "revolutionary cadre" and "revolutionary soldier" backgrounds.[28] "Revisionist" Party cadres, it was further claimed, had practised and preached a "rightist" version of the "class policy" by neglecting the importance of class origin in assessing and advancing young people and by putting exclusive reliance on the behavioural standard.[29] Even the behavioural standards had been lax, it was alleged, and a pun became current to the effect that, in educational recruitment policy, *chung-tsai piao-mien* ("stress on superficial appearance") had been substituted for *chung-tsai piao-hsien* ("stress on [political] behaviour"), thus allowing phoney progressives from dubious family origins to get into universities. The Peking Party Committee was also accused of distorting the "class policy" in YCL recruitment in Peking.[30]

---

27. "The Central Committee of the CCP and the State Council decide to reform the methods of enrolment to higher level schools," *KMJP*, June 18, 1966; "The twenty-one great crimes of the system of educational recruitment through exams," *KMJP*, June 19, 1966; "*People's Daily* editorial on the importance of transforming the Chinese educational system," NCNA, Peking, June 18, 1966, in *SCMP* No.3724, pp.13-16.
28. For example, see a collection of such articles translated in *Union Research Service* (hereafter *URS*), Vol.44, No.1.
29. "We have definitely taken the road of revolution," *Ta-kung Pao* [Impartial Daily] (hereafter *TKP*), Peking, June 19, 1966, p.2, trans. in *URS*, Vol.44, No.1.
30. For a report on these alleged misdeeds, see "The new YCL City Committee holds its first plenary session," NCNA, July 26, 1966, in *SCMP* No.3756, pp.3-4.

Mass involvement in this phase of the movement was almost exclusively confined to "reliable" students of "good" class origins: worker-peasant youth, YCL or Party members and the children of Party, government and armed forces cadres of which Peking, being the administrative capital, had an abundance. They were reacting forcefully against the perceived liberalisation of class criteria over the past two years which they regarded as ideologically unsound and damaging to their interests. The charges current in the media clearly reflected their attitudes and interests. Some of the polemics were written by middle school students from "red" family origins. For example, students from the senior graduation class of Peking No.4 Middle School, one of the two schools whose students raised the original proposal to change college enrolment procedures, made the following allegations:

> The bourgeois sirs in "authority" boast of their children as "fine porcelain" which looks pretty even without any flowery design on it. They viciously curse the children of workers and peasants as "coarse chinaware" which simply cannot be made pretty by any painting... Those agents of the bourgeoisie who have sneaked into our party have tried to use this invisible sword of the entrance exams to mercilessly cut off the path leading the children of labouring people to the pinnacles of science and culture... They have...done their best to discriminate against and obstruct the children of workers, poor and lower-middle peasants, revolutionary cadres and revolutionary soldiers.[31]

It was alleged that too many children of bad family origins had gained entrance to better colleges in the early and mid-1960's because "they took no interest in politics and buried themselves in study." When youth of good family origin did succeed in entering university, it was further claimed, it was more likely to be an inferior institution. Students in the provinces echoed the Peking students with their own complaints. For example, students at the Shansi Province Institute of Finance and Economics lamented the meritocratic admissions criteria in force before the Cultural Revolution and the consequent stratification of educational institutions:

---

31. "We have definitely taken the road of revolution," *TKP*, June 19, 1966, in *URS*, Vol.44, No.1.

> The old entrance examination system for enrolling students divided the schools into higher and lower, noble and mean, classes and grades. Those who gained high marks would be permitted to enter some "special," "key" or "popular brand" schools, while others who got lower marks could only enter ordinary schools. Some of our fellow students were once restless in their study because they were admitted to this "nameless" Institute of Finance and Economics.[32]

Teachers and administrators in middle schools and colleges were accused of "lacking class feelings for the children of workers and peasants" and of trying to embarrass, humiliate and even expel them. A Canton middle school teacher, for example, was criticised for giving 90 percent for an essay by a non-proletarian youth which criticised the peasantry and only 55 percent for one written by a cadre's child describing the study of Mao's thoughts in farm labour.[33] In Peking, bitter criticism was heaped on Lu P'ing, the President and Party Secretary of Peking University, who was accused of regarding worker-peasant students as "teacups that leak" and of using the method of "passing bowels" to "discharge" them from Peking University.[34]

It is clear that the middle school students involved in the movement in this period were preoccupied with the task of getting to college. Given the stress on academic achievement in the old admission system, with its implicit bias against working-class youth, an increase in the stress on political and class criteria was clearly to their advantage. There was the hope abroad among many students from "good" origins, moreover, that active participation in the Cultural Revolution would qualify them for college admission. This was an incentive to restrict recruitment to the emerging new mass organisations.

---

32. "Resolutely beat down the old evil examination system of enrolment," *TKP*, June 20, 1966, p.2, in *URS*, Vol.44, No.1.
33. *Yang-ch'eng Wan-pao* [Yang-ch'eng Evening News], Canton, June 24, 1966, in *SCMP* No.3740, p.14.
34. K'ung Fan, "Lu P'ing's revisionist line and its evil consequences," *JMJP*, July 19, 1966, in *SCMP* No.3751, pp.13-20.

Although the charges levelled against P'eng Chen and various educational administrators were clearly exaggerated, the proposed strengthening of the "class line" in educational placement would have adversely affected all youth outside that group of "good" class origins known as the "five reds" (*hung wu lei*) (worker, poor and lower-middle peasant, revolutionary cadre, revolutionary armyman, revolutionary martyr). Within the non-"five red" category, we should emphasise the distinction between those of "bad" or "exploiting class" origins (such as "landlord," "capitalist" or "counter-revolutionary") and those of "middling" origins (such as "free professional," "employee" or "petty capitalist"). As we have seen in the Introduction, youth of "middling" family origins had been more formidable competitors for the "five reds" than those of "exploiting class" origin whose access to higher education had been gradually declining in the years after the liberalisation period of 1960 to 1962. Jealousy of the "middling" group was visible, for example, in "five red" fulminations against "putting marks in command" and in this attack on Lu P'ing:

> The Lu P'ing black gang said: "In future the superiority in intellectual circles will be held not by worker-peasant children but by children of high intellectuals and employees."[35]

In July, this kind of complaint and criticism gradually crystallised into an ideological position expressing the interests and attitudes of many youth from "five red" origins. According to this position, class origin was the key determinant of the political character of youth: in short, political vice or virtue was inherited. This position seems to have been promoted most forcefully by the sons and daughters of high-ranking civilian and military cadres ("revolutionary cadres" and "revolutionary armymen") in Peking middle schools. This point of view is evident in a leaflet written in mid-July by a student from the middle school attached to Tsinghua University, the source of the first "Red

---

35. *Ibid.*, p.17.

Guard" organisations.[36] The author called on youth of "five red" origins to organise their "class forces" and to "carry forward the class line according to *ch'eng-fen*." The majority of "five red" youth, he argued, had "correct thoughts and correct behaviour" while non-"five red" youth were opportunists, intellectual exhibitionists and obsequious bookworms who longed to become "experts" and "professors" with consumer comforts, fat salaries, high prestige and "political capital." The leaflet cited a traditional proverb to express the idea of inherited class characteristics: "In contact with vermilion, one becomes red; in contact with ink, one becomes black." Though it was possible, in theory, for youth of bad family origin to attain acceptable levels of political behaviour, the author admitted, this required a superhuman effort of self-transformation: they had to "draw out their guts and change their bones." Given the innate political superiority of "five red" youth, he concluded, they should be guaranteed the lion's share of social and political opportunities, apparently at the expense of both "middling" and "bad" origin youth: "*We* will fill your posts in culture, science and technology. Your monopolies are broken."

A later chronology of the early stages of the Cultural Revolution, published by a "rebel" source in early 1967, states that this one-sided emphasis on the importance of family origin appeared in late July 1966.[37] At first, it was not presented in systematic form, existing more as a patchwork of arguments and slogans. In August, as we shall see in the next section, it was to be rephrased and synthesised by a college student named T'an Li-fu. In the latter months of 1966, it was dubbed "only origin theory" (*wei ch'u-shen lun*)

---

36. Ch'i Hsiang-tung, "Hail, line of the proletarian class!" printed by Ch'ih P'iao middle school of the Peking College for Petroleum Industry, trans. in *China News Analysis*, No.636, November 11, 1966.
37. "The Great Proletarian Cultural Revolution: a record of major events," a February 1967 Red Guard document trans. in *Joint Publications Research Service: Political and Sociological Translations on Communist China* (hereafter *JPRS:PS*), No.420 (42,349), August 25, 1967.

or "blood pedigree theory" (*hsüeh-t'ung lun*) by its "rebel" opponents. In July and early August, however, the idea of inter-generationally transmitted political characteristics was expressed by a slogan in the form of a couplet (*tui-lien*) of the kind used traditionally to flank doors and adorn lintels. Hence the slogan came to be known simply as the "couplet" or, to its later "rebel" critics, the "reactionary couplet." The first two stanzas were as follows:

> If the old man's a hero, the son's a good chap,
> If the old man's a reactionary, the son's a bad egg.

In a speech to Red Guards in August, Chiang Ch'ing traced this to a line in a well known Peking opera. The message of the couplet was similar to that of a traditional popular saying:

> A dragon gives birth to a dragon; a phoenix gives birth to a phoenix; but the son of a rat can only burrow holes.

The couplet's third stanza had a variety of forms: sometimes it was the more moderate *chi-pen ju-ts'u*, "this is *basically* so," sometimes the more extreme *chüeh-tui ju-ts'u*, "this is *absolutely* so." These variations imply that supporters of the couplet disagreed among themselves as to exactly how much emphasis should be placed on class origin and how much room should be left for the behavioural criterion of political rectitude. There was also an alternative to the slogan's crude bipolar division of youth in the form of another couplet which distinguished *three* groups of youth:

> If the old man's a hero, the son's a good chap; if the old man's just ordinary, the son sits on the fence; if the old man's a reactionary, the son's a bad egg.

This version implied that youth from "middling" family origins were vacillating middle-of-the-roaders who thus could not be trusted in spite of their academic excellence. It is important to stress these variations and the probable existence of "moderate" and "extreme" versions of this kind of thinking, because later "rebel" critiques have cast it into a crude stereotyped mould of "blood pedigree theory."

The couplet in its various forms was a major source of disagreement and mutual recrimination in Peking's middle schools and colleges, especially the former, in late July and early August. This was the period of the "Fifty Days" when Party work teams came to schools and colleges to guide the movement. The activities of the work-teams seem to have implicitly fostered the growth of "blood pedigree" type thinking among students: they concentrated on mobilising primarily youths of good class origin, notably the children of cadres; they conceptualised the "class struggle" of the Cultural Revolution in terms of "old" class definitions which led them to direct attacks against people with bad *ch'eng-fen*; and they used class *ch'eng-fen* and class origin as weapons to discredit their opponents.

Among the top CCP leadership, however, reactions to the new current of "blood pedigree theory" varied and these variations reflected wider differences of opinion on the purposes of the Cultural Revolution and its future course. Party leaders such as T'ao Chu, Liu Shao-ch'i and T'an Ch'en-lin, while not explicitly supporting "blood pedigree theory," were favourably inclined towards its ideological logic and the political process it reflected. They gave encouragement to the "five red" student groups by stressing the continued importance of class *ch'eng-fen* and family origin. In an August 2nd meeting with Red Guards held at the People's University, for example, T'ao Chu was clearly concerned to avoid making a comment on the validity of the "couplet." Instead, he called on the audience to consult Chairman Mao's previous statements on the issue and asked them not to pressure him into an answer.[38] Later in the month, however, in a speech to Red Guards from the Central-South region, he took a position which leaned towards that of the "couplet" in the degree of political importance he attached to class origin:

> What type of people join the "Red Guards?" Much depends on the class origin of these people. If they are from families of irreproachable origin, they are always better than those from families of questionable origin. We should take class status into account first, but this is not the only criterion. First, we should

---

38. "Comrade T'ao Chu's August 2 speech at the People's University," in *Current Background* (hereafter *CB*), No.830, p.16.

> judge people primarily by their class status; second, we should avoid doing so on a purely class status basis; third, we should put the stress on political behaviour. But to talk all the time about putting the stress on behaviour is revisionism.[39]

T'an Ch'en-lin, a vice premier and the Party leader with primary responsibility for agriculture, laid a heavy emphasis on the need for Red Guards to be recruited from "five red" students.[40] Li Hsüeh-feng, who was involved in the reorganisation of the Peking YCL apparatus during this period, also laid great stress on the inherited "class character" of youth.[41] Liu Shao-ch'i saw the movement mainly as an effort to mobilise politically reliable students against bad "old" class elements and a small group of errant cadres. Although he cautioned Red Guards in early August not to assume that *all* youth with bad family origins were enemies of socialism, thus repudiating implicitly the crude determinism of the "couplet," he was clearly not in favour of Red Guard organisations recruiting large numbers of youth of non-"five red" origin.[42] During this period he maintained that the new organisations should be led and manned by "reliable" youth, notably Party and League members who would be overwhelmingly of "five red" origin. His caution to the Red Guards on the issue of class was thus a question of tactics: too bitter an antagonism would provoke unnecessary resentment and opposition.

If these leading Party cadres fostered the emergence of "blood pedigree theory," consciously or unconsciously, explicitly or implicitly, key "radical" leaders in the Central Committee's Cultural Revolution Group (CRG) took a critical attitude from the outset. They saw this kind of attitude as,

---

39. "Comrade T'ao Chu's speech at the CCP Central Committee's Department of Propaganda," August 25, 1966, in *CB* No.819, pp.13-14.
40. "The [capitalist] powerholders and only origin theory," *Chung-hsüeh Wen-ko Pao* [Middle School Cultural Revolution News], April 1, 1967.
41. *Ibid.*
42. For example, see Liu's "Talk to the Great Proletarian Cultural Revolution Corps," August 3, 1966, in *Collected Works of Liu Shao-ch'i 1958-1967* (Hong Kong: Union Research Institute, 1968), pp.335-39.

at best, well-intentioned but crude fanaticism, at worst an attempt to direct the movement from its real targets ("new" class elements *within* the Party) towards relatively unimportant ones ("old" class elements *outside* the Party). Ch'en Po-ta, head of the CRG, became embroiled in a heated debate with students over the wording of the couplet which showed that his conception of the purpose and scope of the Cultural Revolution was very different from that of Liu, T'ao, Li or T'an. In visits to the middle school attached to Peking Normal University and Tsinghua University in early August he was questioned on the subject. He described the debate at Tsinghua as follows:

> [The students] told me that a worker had changed the couplet to read: "When the old man's a revolutionary, the son tries hard to be a hero; when the father is reactionary, the son should rebel"... Chairman Mao has said that "to rebel is justified." Hence, *if the father is reactionary, the son should rebel*. People have argued with me because of what I've said. Probably everyone's against me.[43]

Ch'en was thus supporting the right of *all* youth, regardless of class background, to participate in the Cultural Revolution by "rebelling" and thus was implicitly questioning the way in which the mass movement had been conducted by the Party work teams.

Another leading "radical" Maoist, K'ang Sheng, also criticised the "couplet" in early August, calling on middle school Red Guards in Peking to use the "class policy" correctly by basing it on Mao's 1964 description of the five qualities necessary for "revolutionary successors."[44] Since none of Mao's five criteria mentioned class origin, K'ang was thus emphasising the primacy of the *behavioural* definition of class. Chiang Ch'ing took a comparable line to Ch'en and K'ang in opposing the couplet. Like Ch'en, she argued that

---

43. "Comrade Ch'en Po-ta's talk to students at the reception room of the Cultural Revolution Group under the CCP Central Committee at noon on August 5," in *CB* No.830, p.22 (emphasis added).
44. "Comrade K'ang Sheng's speech to middle school Red Guards and Red Flag Combat Groups in Peking at Tienchiao Theatre on August 6," in *CB* No.819, p.9.

the couplet's second stanza should be amended to read "When parents are reactionaries, their children should *rebel*."[45] The original couplet, in her opinion, was a traditional relic and should be repudiated since "such old feudal terminology cannot express a new thought." The correct approach to such questions, she maintained, lay in the understanding that the correct "class policy" emphasised political behaviour as the major standard for judging a young person's political qualities.

These disagreements over the issue of class origin and its relation to Red Guard recruitment were symptomatic of a deeper struggle which was emerging between "moderate" and "radical" leaders at the Party centre. The "radicals" wanted to push the movement on to a new stage, converting it from a Party machine-directed undertaking, raking over the coals of "old" class antagonisms, into a new form of class struggle where the scope of participants expanded beyond those people deemed reliable by the Party machine and where the primary focus of struggle was on "class enemies" at high levels in the Party. The class issues which had dominated this first stage thus had different meanings for the opposing groups within the leadership. For the "moderate" (or "revisionist") Party leaders and their followers among the masses, the movement served a "progressive" purpose in reinforcing the "class line" in university and Youth League recruitment and in defending the gains of the revolution against its traditional enemies and their offspring. The "radicals," on the other hand, while sharing the view that the redistributive aspects of the "class line" had to be strengthened, felt that these issues were increasingly being used as a means to avoid the basic issues of the campaign which involved the "new" class structure rather than the "old."

The Eleventh Plenum of the CCP Central Committee in early August broke the deadlock and moved the campaign in the direction that the "radicals" desired. The Decision of the

---

45. "A talk by Comrade Chiang Ch'ing to the Red Guard fighters on August 6, 1966," in *CB* No.830, pp.24-25 (emphasis added).

Plenum set the movement in the context of a "new" political class struggle directed against "capitalist roaders" within the Party but still left enough ambiguity in its discussion of "the Party's class line" to provide scope for disagreement on the application of "class" categories to concrete political action.[46] The Decision began a new stage in the Cultural Revolution, lasting from late August to the end of the year, which involved a seesaw struggle between "rebels" and "conservatives." We now turn to the role played by the notion of "class" and the issue of class origin during this period.

Phase 2 - August-December 1966: "Rebels" vs. "Conservatives"

At the ideological level, the debate continued during this period on the question of which definition of "class" was appropriate to the movement. The answer was crucial to the nature of the struggle taking place within the central leadership and among educated urban youth. New groups of "rebel" Red Guards emerged which, under the prompting of key "radical" figures in the Central Cultural Revolution Group, espoused the behavioural view of "class" thus legitimising "class struggle" against the "capitalist roaders" in the Party. In this second phase, "rebel" critics linked the initial "five red" Red Guard groups of July and August with the discredited Party work teams, accused them of advocating the extreme position of "blood pedigree theory" and of defending the "revisionist" Party officials under attack. Hence, in "rebel" terminology, they were labelled as "conservatives." Red Guard activities expanded beyond Peking during this period and a heated mass debate developed between rival groups on the issue of class. By the end of the year, the "rebel" groups and their representatives at the Centre had gained temporary ideological and political predominance.

The ideological situation in August was still somewhat ambiguous. The Decision of the CCP Central Committee on the

---

46. For an English text, see K.H. Fan, ed., *The Chinese Cultural Revolution: Selected Documents* (New York, N.Y.: Grove Press, 1968), pp.162-73.

Cultural Revolution appeared to favour a political-behavioural definition of "class" and "class enemies" but failed to mention the controversy over the "couplet." Thus on the question of recruitment to the Red Guards, the text was unspecific enough to support a variety of positions on the issue. Indeed, the early "five red" Red Guard group appeared to receive a boost from no less a person than Mao himself when he gave his public blessing to the Red Guards on August 18th. By attending their parade and allowing them to tie a red armband on his arm, he was in fact sanctioning organisations composed of "five red" youth. Apart from the Peking contingent, over 100,000 students from other cities also attended the rally and these too were overwhelmingly "five red" youth. In fact, the Red Guards were defined for the occasion as "an organisation set up by middle school pupils from the families of worker, former poor and lower-middle peasants, revolutionary cadres and revolutionary armymen."[47]

Since the Cultural Revolution had taken a turn more threatening to the "revisionist" Party elite, the definition of "class" and "class struggle" became crucial for both "conservatives" who wanted to rein in the movement and "radicals" who wanted to push on. Party leaders under attack found it difficult to swim against an ideological tide increasingly dominated by "radical" thinking. They were increasingly unable to articulate their own views openly and relied on the activities and arguments of Red Guard groups sympathetic to their position, i.e. the first wave of "five red" organisations, particularly the organisations formed by the children of high-ranking cadres. These mass groups shared both an ideological affinity and a common interest with threatened cadres. For the "conservative" leaders and mass organisations as for the "radicals," the basic issues were

---

47. "Chairman Mao joins revolutionary masses in celebration of the Great Proletarian Cultural Revolution," NCNA, Peking, August 18, 1966, in *SCMP* No.3766, p.6; "A million-strong parade in Peking celebrates the Great Proletarian Cultural Revolution," *ibid.*, p.9.

perceived in terms of "class." Veteran Party leaders, such as Liu Shao-ch'i, they felt, were "advanced elements of the proletariat" and to attack them was to commit a counter-revolutionary act. In the mass movement, moreover, if the base of recruitment was widened as the "radicals" demanded to include youth of "impure" origins and if these "impure" elements were allowed, nay encouraged, to attack Party cadres, then this was tantamount in their eyes to allowing the defeated "old" class enemies to wreak "class revenge." The "conservative" leaders took their stand on what they saw as a legitimate structure of political power and a correct definition of "class," positions which the "radicals" perceived as an ideological smokescreen to protect "new class" interests. The imputation was overly Machiavellian. This was a clear confrontation between consistent ideological positions as well as opposing sets of socio-political interests.

Thus the questions of whether or not "five red" youth were in fact "reliable" and whether or not high-ranking cadres under attack were representatives of the "proletariat" were, for "conservative" cadres and masses, two aspects of the same issue. On August 20, the two themes were fused in a speech by T'an Li-fu, a student at the Peking Engineering University and son of a deceased high-ranking cadre in the political-legal system.[48] In this speech, T'an is described as having defended the central tenets of "blood pedigree theory" in the area of Red Guard recruitment and as having vouched for the revolutionary qualities of leading Party cadres then coming under attack. In the words of a later "rebel" critique, T'an's speech was politically important because "he has said what the bourgeois faction in authority dare not say themselves." In his talks, T'an opposed what he called the "impeachment" of high officials such as Liu Shao-ch'i and "compared the impeachment of certain persons to bowing out by the

---

48. For "rebel" critiques of T'an's speech, see "Look at the true visage of Mount Lu," Hung Wei Ping [Red Guard], No. 11, November 16, 1966, p.3, in *JPRS:PS* No.391 (40, 488), April 3, 1967; *Materials Relating to the Great Proletarian Cultural Revolution*, Canton, October 28, 1966, pp.37-40, in *JPRS:PS* No.387 (40, 391), March 24, 1967.

proletariat." He called on these cadres to be "firm and unbending" in the face of "rebel" criticism, defended the activities of the Party work teams and argued that only youths of good class background should participate in the Cultural Revolution because they had "class feelings" which made them reliable. In a later rebel account, it is alleged that T'an received both open and covert support from Li Hsüeh-feng and the reorganised Peking City CCP Committee, who helped with the mechanics of reprinting and distributing his speech.[49] His remarks were known as "T'an's talks" and they enjoyed a wide circulation throughout the country. Some schools allegedly printed many thousands of copies and one "rebel" critic complained that, for a while, "T'an's talks" were more conspicuous than the Central Committee's August Decision on the Cultural Revolution.

"T'an's talks" provided a theoretical basis for the "conservative" Red Guard organisations which continued to dominate the mass movement during late August and September. These organisations also received formal or informal support from ranking cadres, in Peking and the provinces, who felt the waves of mass criticism lapping at their feet. The struggle at the intra-leadership level was heavily intertwined with struggle at the mass level during the labyrinthine turmoil of late 1966: central and local leaders were attacking each other and taking opposing political stands; they were sending out conflicting messages to the basic levels; they were egging on Red Guard groups against rival groups and against their opponents within the leadership. The Red Guards, in turn, responded to cues from above in complex and often unpredictable ways and the logic of their own struggle with opposing groups intertwined with the logic of conflict at the various ascending levels of leadership above them. To simplify matters, I shall deal first with the ways in which various central leaders intervened to shape the emerging process of mass politics during this period and then focus on the process of Red Guard politics itself.

---

49. *Chung-hsüeh Wen-ko Pao*, April 1, 1967.

(*i*) "Class" and Leadership Conflict

Since the central leaders under attack could not express their positions publicly, we cannot document their views on the class-related issues in dispute in this period. It seems reasonable to assume, however, that their opinions coincided to a large extent with those of T'an Li-fu. There is more information available, however, on the positions taken by those central leaders who were engaged in directing and managing the movement, notably Chou En-lai and Ch'en Po-ta.

Chou En-lai seems to have played the role of moderator between the attempts by both "conservatives" and "rebels" to redefine class-related policies, attempting in each case to reaffirm the definitions and practices current before the Cultural Revolution. In September and early October, he devoted considerable effort to correcting the excesses of the "five red" Red Guard groups (for these, see the next subsection) and he intervened on several occasions to discuss the issue of Red Guard recruitment. Since he took his stand on the basis of the pre-Cultural Revolution "class policy," he too reflected its ambiguity. On the one hand, he emphasised the behavioural criterion. He affirmed that non-"five red" students could not choose the family into which they were born; that the primary criterion of evaluation should be "objective political acts" not family origin; that as long as children of non-"five red" origin had "turned their backs on their original class," they should be admitted to Red Guard organisations.[50] He made the pragmatic point, moreover, that if Red Guard membership were restricted to the "five reds," then a majority of college students and a near majority of middle school students would not be able to participate in the Cultural Revolution. As a result, a new contradiction would develop between those admitted and those excluded.[51] More

---

50. "Premier Chou En-lai's speech to representatives of Peking's 'Red Guards'," in *CB* No.819, pp.16ff.; "Speech by Premier Chou En-lai," September 25, 1966, in Thomas W. Robinson, ed., *The Cultural Revolution in China* (Berkeley, Calif.: University of California Press, 1971), Appendix B, pp.302-03.
51. "Speech by Premier Chou at the Altar of Agriculture Park on September 13, 1966," in *CB* No.819, pp.45-46.

fundamentally, he criticised the very notion of "five reds" and, by inference, its theoretical matrix, "blood pedigree" thinking. He made this clear in a talk to Red Guard representatives from the Harbin Engineering Institute in early October:

> You are called the "five red categories." There are also "five black categories." If it isn't red then it's black. This is a sort of absolutisation of concept which is very dangerous. Even if a person has made a mistake, his children cannot be called one of the black categories. This would become fatalism (*su-ming-lun*). Chairman Mao opposes this... absolutisation is not the thought of Mao.[52]

He also criticised the idea of the "seven black elements," which had been coined by the "five reds" to define their enemies, arguing that the proposal to add "capitalist" as an extra "black" *ch'eng-fen* was an unwarranted revision of united front policies.[53] He chided the "five red" Red Guards for the "narrow-mindedness" of their demand for the abolition of ballet on the grounds that "most of those who enjoy ballet do not belong to the five red categories," or the demand that ballet performers should all be from "five red" origins. The political tactics of the "five reds," according to Chou, also left a lot to be desired:

> You are very young and have one belief, i.e. you first call someone a "bad egg" and then invite him to come over to your side if he wants to make revolution. Of course, it is all right to use a few offensive words. We older people regard them in a one dividing into two manner. But to younger people they are not so tolerable. You must pay attention to this.[54]

In spite of these criticisms of the actions and assumptions of the "five red" Red Guards and his reaffirmation of the importance of political behaviour and class origin,

---

52. "Main points of the speech delivered by Chou En-lai to representatives from the Engineering Institute of Harbin," early October, 1966, in *SCMP (Supplement)*, No.159, p.43.
53. "Premier Chou En-lai's speech to representatives of Peking's 'Red Guards'," in *CB* No.819, p.19; "Speech by Premier Chou En-lai," September 25, 1966, in Robinson, *The Cultural Revolution*, Appendix B, p.299.
54. "Speech by Premier Chou En-lai on September 10 at an oath-taking rally of those going out to establish revolutionary ties," in *CB* No.819, p.37.

Chou still attached considerable significance to the factor of family origin. He accepted the idea that the "nucleus" or "main body" of the Red Guards, their leadership and activist core, should be composed of "five reds."[55] Although he supported the recruitment of non-"five reds," he maintained that the recruits should mainly come from youth of "middling" origins (such as middle peasant, upper-middle peasant or handicraftsmen).[56] In short, although Chou En-lai's reiteration of the pre-Cultural Revolution "class policy" repudiated tendencies towards the heterodox "theory of blood pedigree," he did not transcend the ambiguity at the heart of the previous policy.

"Radical" leaders such as Lin Piao, Chiang Ch'ing and Ch'en Po-ta laid great emphasis on the behavioural definition of "class." Ch'en Po-ta played a key role during this period: he criticised T'an Li-fu and the initial Red Guard organisations dominated by cadres' children, identifying them both as expressions of a "new bourgeoisie" and "new privileged stratum."[57] In Ch'en's view, "blood pedigree theory" was mere ideological camouflage for the power interests of this "privileged stratum" and a means of deflecting the focus of political struggle onto relatively harmless scapegoats, people of "bad" class *ch'eng-fen* and origin.[58] Ch'en more than any of the "radical Maoist" group among the central leadership saw class as a question of political behaviour and thought in terms of the "new" class analysis. For Ch'en, the "correct" class line was a question of political orientation, defined in terms of left, right and centre. Young people were to acquire class consciousness through social practice and the study of Mao's works. Their progress was to be measured according to Mao's five criteria for "revolutionary successors" which did not

---

55. *Ibid.*
56. "Speech by Premier Chou at the Altar of Agriculture Park on September 13, 1966," in *CB* No.819, pp.45-46.
57. "Comrade Ch'en Po-ta's summary of two months of the movement," *Tung-feng Chan-pao* [East Wind Combat Bulletin], 2, December 11, 1966, pp.2-3, in *JPRS:PS* No.391 (40, 488), April 3, 1967, p.10.
58. *Ibid.*, p.15.

include the criterion of class origin. He saw the attainment of proletarian consciousness as a long-term process:

> Man must constantly undergo long-term self-inspection through struggle in order to prove which class his world view belongs to. Ideological consciousness is not inborn. It is a reflection of social existence.[59]

The role of Lin Piao and the People's Liberation Army (PLA) was also important in disseminating the behavioural definition of class during this period. A later chronology remarks that the relationship between "blood pedigree theory" and "the struggle between the two lines" did not become clear until the editorial in *Red Flag* and Lin Piao's remarks at the celebration of National Day on October 1st were made public.[60] Both of these documents declared the major targets of the Cultural Revolution to be "new" class enemies, viz. "those in authority in the Party taking the capitalist road." Great emphasis was placed in the media in early October on Lin Piao's call for a mass movement to "study and apply Chairman Mao's works," the implication being that this, rather than family origin, would be the major criterion for recruiting and assessing Red Guards. The same message was conveyed in a speech by Hsiao Hua to a meeting of Air Force cadres and by a *Liberation Army Daily* editorial on October 11.[61] On October 9, Liu Shih of the *Liberation Army Daily* criticised T'an Li-fu by name[62] and, later in the month, a PLA deputy political instructor was reported as criticising "natural redness" and emphasising that, although "simple class sentiment" is unique to the children of workers and peasants and revolutionary cadres, yet "without raising this to the plane of class consciousness [by the study of Mao's thought], one cannot

---

59. *Ibid.*, pp.15-16.
60. *JPRS: Translations on Communist China*, No.401 (41, 446), June 19, 1967, p.43; for Lin Piao's speech, see *Peking Review*, October 7, 1966, pp.10-11; "Forward along the high road of Mao Tse-tung's Thought," *Hung-ch'i* [Red Flag], No.13, in *ibid.*, pp.15-17.
61. *Peking Review*, October 14, 1966, pp.6-8 and 12-13.
62. *Wu-ch'an chieh-chi wen-hua ta ko-ming yu-kuan ts'ai-liao* [Relevant Materials on the Great Proletarian Cultural Revolution], Canton, October 28, 1966, in *JPRS:PS* No.387 (40, 391), March 24, 1967.

possibly resist the corruption of bourgeois ideology."[63] Another editorial in the *Liberation Army Daily* in late October also stressed that the proletarian world view was not spontaneous and had to be cultivated by studying Mao's works.[64]

It is crucial to be aware, however, that, even though "radical" leaders such as Ch'en and Lin put the primary stress on political behaviour in the context of a "new" class analysis, at no point did they take the position that "old" class *ch'eng-fen* or family origin were unimportant or irrelevant. Even Ch'en Po-ta, who seems to have been the most extreme advocate of class as a political-ideological phenomenon, was careful to preface his remarks with the caveat that "it is wrong not to stress class origin" and the reminder that "Chairman Mao and the Party lay great stress on rearing elements of good class origin."[65] PLA commentaries on the issue, moreover, declared that a good class origin was an advantage, since it created raw "class sentiment" which facilitated the attainment of proletarian consciousness.[66]

There were several reasons for this continuing ambiguity on the part of "radical" leaders. First, in ideological terms, it was felt that the correct Maoist position involved *both* principles of class definition, the key problem not being "either/or" but one of relative emphasis. To jettison either would have been heretical. Second, in political terms, it would have been as unwise for the radicals to deny the importance of class *ch'eng-fen* and origin as it would have for their opponents to deny the importance of the behavioural

---

63. "Transform people's souls with the Thought of Mao Tse-tung - a talk by a deputy political instructor of a certain PLA unit, Wang Tao-ming," *JMJP*, October 25, 1966, in *SCMP* No.3814, p.4.
64. "The necessary road to the revolutionisation of thinking," *Chieh-fang Chün-pao* [Liberation Army Daily] editorial, NCNA, October 25, 1966, in *SCMP* No.3814, pp.12-13.
65. "Comrade Ch'en Po-ta's summary of two months of the movement," *loc.cit.*, pp.15-16.
66. "Transform people's souls with the Thought of Mao Tse-tung - a talk by a deputy political instructor of a certain PLA unit, Wang Tao-ming," *JMJP*, October 25, 1966, in *SCMP* No.3814, p.4.

criterion: this would have opened them up to charges of having "no firm class standpoint," of lack of concern for the workers and peasants, of aiding the "five elements," etc. Third, there was uncertainty about where to go if the "old" class labels were in fact jettisoned. How could society be recategorised in a way which would be both ideologically correct and politically acceptable? This uncertainty can be detected in statements of three important "radical" theorists, Kuan Feng, Wang Li and Ch'i Pen-yü, in speeches to Red Guards in October. They clearly regarded the "old" system of demarcation as inappropriate to the changing situation, but were unable to provide an alternative mode of classification. Wang Li expressed his uncertainty as follows:

> Does it mean we do not care about a person's origin? No, it doesn't. We must define family origin in scientific terms. Taking a worker, poor and lower-middle peasant, revolutionary cadre or revolutionary soldier, we do not mean that when these terms are abolished, the factor of class origin is also abolished. No, we do not mean that. The question is this: how can we define class status more scientifically?[67]

Given this continuing recognition of "old" class categories on the part of the major "radical" leaders, they were not prepared to accept a new heterodoxy which emerged from among the "rebel" mass organisations in late 1966. This new doctrine argued the opposite case to "blood pedigree theory:" that, in evaluating the political qualities and "class stand" of youth, class origin should be regarded as *irrelevant*. Named "origin theory" by its proponents, this new analysis became the topic of large-scale debate among Red Guard groups in early 1967. Before discussing this development, however, I shall first describe briefly the evolving process of mass politics on the issue of class origin during the period from August to December 1966.

(*ii*) Mass Politics: "Rebel" vs. "Conservative" Red Guards

If the decline of the influence of "blood pedigree theory" in late 1966 coincided with shifts in the balance of power

---

67. *SCMM (Supplement)* No.15, May 8, 1967, p.15.

between central leaders, it also saw realignments among the new mass organisations. Although the initial wave of Red Guard groups, organised in July and early August under the auspices of the Party work teams, were dominant in late August and September, they gradually lost ground to the "rebels" who had temporarily gained the upper hand by December.

In late August and September, the major political thrust still came from the Peking Red Guards who were dominated by the children of high-ranking political and military cadres. Peking was their major power base because of the high concentration of Party and government cadres there and the consequent development of various institutions designed to service them and their families. They were well represented in Peking's prestigious colleges, notably Peking and Tsinghua universities. At Tsinghua, for example, there were estimated to be 49 children of senior "revisionist" cadres attacked during the Cultural Revolution, including children of Liu Shao-ch'i, Li Ching-ch'uan, P'eng Chen, Hu K'o-shih and Wang Jen-chung.[68] Certain middle schools in the city were well known both for their intellectual quality and for their high concentration of children of "revolutionary cadres."[69] Senior cadres' children tended to accumulate in the "attached middle schools" linked to universities or colleges, or in special schools for cadres' children, notably the August 1st middle school. These institutions had provided most of the recruits for the urban-district based "inspection teams" which were later to amalgamate to form the most infamous of the cadres' children organisations, the "United Action Committee."[70]

---

68. "Letters from Peking," *Hung-ch'i T'ung-hsün* [Red Flag Bulletin], Canton, No.1, mid-June, 1968.
69. For an example, see the case of Peking University's Attached Middle School in "Smash the revisionist system of 'attached middle schools'," Peking, *Chung-hsüeh Tou-p'i-kai* [Struggle, Criticism and Reform in Middle Schools] 1st issue, June 19, 1967, in *SCMP (Supplement)* No.200, pp.19-23.
70. For example, see "Completely smash the 'United Action Committee', a rightist black organisation," Peking, *Ching-kang-shan* [Chingkang Mountains], January 23, 1967, in *SCMP* No.3905, p.13. For an account of its origins, see "See what kind of goods the 'United Action Committee of the Capital's Red Guards' is," *ibid.*, p.18.

Late August and early September was a period when the ideas implicit in both "blood pedigree theory" and "T'an's talks" were carried to extremes by these and other "five red" Red Guard organisations. Apart from attempting to establish the idea of "five red" as a formal category, they extended the number of "bad" *ch'eng-fen* and family origins from the original "five elements" current before the Cultural Revolution (i.e. landlords, rich peasants, counter-revolutionaries, bad elements and rightists) to the "seven black elements" (*hei ch'i lei*) by adding "capitalists" and, interchangeably, members of the "black gang" or "snakes, demons and monsters," the latter two categories being the major targets of the first stage of the Cultural Revolution from June to August.

Their views on class found expression in a wave of extreme measures designed to "purify" society and to ensure that people of different *ch'eng-fen* and class origins received correspondingly different treatment. For example, the "five red" organisation of the Peking No.26 Middle School issued "One Hundred Examples of Breaking Down the Old and Establishing the New." The examples included the following:

> 32. Laundries must refuse to launder trousers, skirts, socks, stockings and handkerchiefs for the bourgeoisie, their wives, sons and daughters, so as to smash their evil fashion.
>
> 33. Bath houses must not serve the bourgeoisie nor massage them.
>
> 37. The bourgeoisie are not allowed to hire nursing maids.
>
> 46. Except for the old, weak and disabled, the bourgeoisie are not allowed to use pedicabs.
>
> 49. The bourgeoisie can use restaurants but service personnel cannot prepare elaborate meals for them, nor are they allowed to play the finger guessing game there.
>
> 50. Landlords, rich peasants, counter-revolutionaries, bad elements and rightists working in factories are not to be given retirement gratuities.
>
> 52. An unemployed member of the "five categories" must go to the countryside.

63. Cars, TVs and motor cycles owned by the "five categories" and members of the black gang should be confiscated and given to street committees for entertaining the family members of the workers and peasants.[71]

A person resident in Peking at the time listed several examples of class discrimination during this phase of the movement: when a person went into a restaurant, he or she had to fill in a form stating class origin; people with bad individual class status were not welcome on buses so they had to pretend to be workers; a doctor of bourgeois background would be afraid to do an operation on a working class person in case it failed whereupon he might be accused of "class revenge." Later "rebel" Red Guard media gave other examples of the excesses of this period in Peking "when the T'an Li-fu line was prevalent." At the traditional Chinese medicine hospital, for instance, some outpatients were asked to divulge their individual class status. If, for example, the patient belonged to the "black gang" he or she would not be admitted.[72] Another prevalent tendency was for Red Guard organisations to issue directives ordering undesirable class and political elements to vacate the capital. On August 23, for example, the East Is Red Combat Group of the Peking Survey and Design College of the Hydro-Electricity Ministry issued a "final dispatch" to the "four elements (landlords, rich peasants, counter-revolutionaries and bad elements) among family dependents," ordering them to "clear out" of Peking and return to the countryside to undergo mass supervision in their home production brigades.[73]

In late August and September, members of these initial "five red" organisations in Peking fanned out across the country to "make revolutionary liaison" with Red Guards in the provincial cities. In Canton, for example, Red Guards from the Peking Medical College were described as communicating

---

71. September 1, 1966, in *SCMM* No.566, pp.12-20.
72. "Indictment by Comrade T'ang Hsi-yang," *How Vicious*, July 1967, in *SCMM* No.618, p.17.
73. A copy of this "dispatch" from the Union Research Institute files, Hong Kong, is in the possession of the author.

their experiences in carrying out the "class line" to students at the Chungshan Medical College.[74] "Five red" youth were the "backbone force" in the Red Guard movement, they argued, so it was important to rouse them by "stimulating their class hatred against the Kuomintang and the exploiting classes." Students from Peking's middle schools were carrying a similar message to their counterparts in Canton. "Five red" students all over the country, they declared, were "melons growing on the same vine" who must "never forget their class sufferings."[75] A branch of the Peking organisation of cadres' children was established in Canton under the name of the Mao Tse-tungism Red Guards (Ism Guards, for short).[76] Like its parent organisation, it was dominated by cadres' children, with the son of Huang Yung-sheng, Commander of the Canton Military Region, as its major leader. Many of its members came from the special school for the children of military cadres in Canton, the August 1st Middle School. The Ism Guards were the major exponents of "blood pedigree theory" in Canton but, owing to the lower concentration of "revolutionary cadres" in Canton and the relatively small percentage of industrial workers among the population (Canton was a veritable sea of "petty bourgeoisie"), the theory had less popular appeal than in Peking.

In September and October, however, the influence of the "five red" groups in Peking and the provincial cities went into decline for several reasons. As we have seen, their ideological premises, implicit support for the previous power structure and narrow recruitment criteria came under increasing criticism from central leaders, including Chou En-lai, Lin Piao, Chiang Ch'ing and Ch'en Po-ta. The new turn in the direction of the campaign towards an attack on "capitalist

---

74. "Red Guards of Peking and Canton emulate and encourage each other," Canton, *Hung Wei Pao* [Red Guard News], September 9, 1966, in *SCMP* No.3783, p.12.
75. "Revolutionary teachers and students in Canton unite with revolutionary teachers and students from other parts of the country to make revolution," Canton, *Hung Wei Pao*, September 27, 1966, in *SCMP* No.3795, p.2.
76. Bennett and Montaperto, *Red Guard*, p.70.

roaders" within the Party gave rise to a new wave of self-defined "rebel" Red Guard groups. The "rebel" nucleus consisted of students who had clashed with the Party work teams in July and, in the latter months of 1966, they were joined by motley groups of students who, for ideological or personal reasons, held grudges against the previous authority structure and/or the early Red Guard groups. The original Red Guards were thus forced onto the defensive, defined invidiously as "conservatives" and compromised by their former (and in some cases continuing) relationship with "revisionist" cadres. As the new "rebel" groups formed, moreover, the solidarity of the "five reds" was weakened. Youths of good origin had been among those who fell foul of the work teams and they assumed the leadership positions in the new "rebel" organisations. They were quick to exploit, moreover, the latent divergences of interest and outlook between the "elite" children of cadres within the "five reds" and the "ordinary" worker-peasant children. The ideological appeal, and political wedge, to pry these two elements apart was the charge that cadres' children were part of a "privileged stratum" which should be opposed by all revolutionary youths, regardless of class background. As student organisations proliferated, moreover, the original "five red" Red Guards found their ability to draw in new recruits constricted by their narrow class-based purism, thus leaving a large number of students, notably those of "middling" origins, available to join "rebel" groups. Moreover, as the movement spread outside Peking, the influence of cadres' children declined since the provincial cities did not have the same high concentration of "revolutionary cadres" as Peking.

Thus, after initially seizing the initiative in August and September, the influence of the "five red" groups declined during October, November and December. Systematic opposition to them began in Peking in late September when a minority of Red Guards in the city's colleges organised a "Committee to defend Mao Tse-tung's Thought and the Sixteen Articles" and held a meeting at the Normal University to criticise

T'an Li-fu.[77] The turning point in the struggle between the two factions seems to have coincided roughly with Lin Piao's speech at the beginning of October. Students at Tsinghua University, for example, who were in the forefront of the movement at the time, date October 6th as "the climax of this struggle, the victory of the rebel line over the loyalist [i.e. conservative] line."[78] After a mass meeting on that date in Tien An Men square, "rebel organisations, morale high, went on the offensive everywhere and conservative organisations began to retreat." From that time on, "blood pedigree theory" was increasingly regarded as a heretical doctrine. Each side tried to discredit the other using "class" concepts. For the "rebels," the "conservatives" were betraying the true interests of the proletariat by protecting "capitalist roaders" in the Party; for the "conservatives," the "rebels" were betraying the interests of the true proletariat by allowing the movement to be subverted by elements of "impure" class status and origin and subjecting the true representatives of the proletariat to counter-revolutionary attack.

Factional struggle over the class issue flared several times in November and early December. On November 8th, "conservative" Red Guards from various educational institutions, including the Peking Foreign Languages Institute, the No.101 Middle School and the attached middle school of the People's University, attacked the "rebel" Third Headquarters with the charge that their ranks were "impure."[79] On November 20th, the same groups attempted to rehabilitate T'an Li-fu and attacked Ch'en Po-ta, Chiang Ch'ing, Kuan Feng and Ch'i Pen-yü who were seen as the main proponents of the "radical" analysis.[80] On November 24th, children from the families of high-ranking

---

77. "The Great Proletarian Cultural Revolution - a record of major events," February 1967, in *JPRS:PS* No.420 (42, 349), August 25, 1967, p.47.
78. William Hinton, "Hundred-Day War: The Cultural Revolution at Tsinghua University," *Monthly Review*, July-August 1972, p.96.
79. "The Great Proletarian Cultural Revolution - a record of major events," February 1967, in *JPRS:PS* No.420 (42, 349), August 25, 1967, p.55.
80. *Ibid.*

cadres at the Peking Aeronautical College allegedly organised an "August 1st Column" to attack the "radicals" in the Central CRG and, on December 1st, a debate was held at the Peking Forestry College where the Central CRG was criticised for labelling T'an Li-fu as a "rightist."[81] In early December, the core "conservative" organisations in Peking, the district-based "Inspection Teams" composed of the children of high cadres, decided to regroup their forces. They inaugurated a new organisation, the "United Action Committee of the Capital's Red Guards" (usually abbreviated to "United Action Committee") with the slogan: "Let the children of revolutionary cadres and revolutionary armymen in the whole city unite!"[82] In mid-December, the radicals in the CRG launched a counter-offensive in coordination with "rebel" groups to dissolve the "conservative" opposition and discredit their class line. Two major radical leaders, Ch'en Po-ta and Chiang Ch'ing, attended a meeting in Peking on December 16th called by the "rebel" Third Headquarters to attack the United Action Committee which was described as the main proponent of "blood pedigree theory" in Peking. Chiang Ch'ing alleged that this organisation of high cadres' children was receiving support from behind the scenes by key central figures such as Chou Jung-hsin (secretary-general of the State Council), Hsü Ming (deputy secretary-general of the State Council) and Yung Wen-tao (secretary of the Peking Municipal Committee Secretariat).[83] A second rally was held in Peking on December 17th and, according to accounts in the "rebel" media, the "conservative" organisations were disbanded. According to later "rebel" accounts, however, "though they dispersed they remained active," and when the opportunity presented itself in the following year, they reasserted their influence in the mass movement.[84]

---

81. *Ibid.*
82. "See what kind of goods the 'United Action Committee of the Capital's Red Guards' is," *Ching-kang-shan*, January 23, 1967, in *SCMP* No.3905, p.19.
83. "New victories of the revolutionary 'Little Red Guard Generals'," *Hung Wei Ping Pao* [Red Guard Bulletin], 15, December 22, 1966, p.1, in *JPRS:PS* No.383 (40, 234), March 13, 1967, p.84.
84. "The Great Proletarian Cultural Revolution - a record of major events," February 1967, in *JPRS:PS* No.420 (42, 349), August 25, 1967.

To summarise, by the end of 1966, under considerable prompting from "radical" leaders in the CRG, the behavioural definition of "class" had become dominant, overshadowing *but not replacing* the "old" socio-economic categories. A heterodox form of class analysis, "blood pedigree theory" or "only origin theory," had been repudiated as heretical. At the level of mass organisations, the original "five red" Red Guards of July and August had been joined *but not displaced* by a heterogeneous collection of "rebel" groups whose leadership tended to be "five red" but whose class composition was somewhat "impure" in that they recruited many non-"five red" youths.

Under the impact of these changes, the debate over class origin and "class policy" took on a different character. The "conservative" Red Guards, who could no longer base their public positions on the crude assumption of "natural redness," moderated their own position somewhat and focused their critical fire on a new heterodoxy which emerged among the "rebel" ranks in late 1966, "origin theory" (*ch'u-shen lun*). The most sophisticated exposition of this theory and the major debates on its validity only appeared in early 1967 during the third phase of our case study.

Phase 3 - Early 1967: "Origin Theory," the "Rebel" Heterodoxy

In the first two months of 1967, the "conservatives" at all levels were on the defensive. In the New Year's editorial in *Red Flag*, "blood pedigree theory" was repudiated as "reactionary historical idealism" which diverted youth of good origin away from the real enemies, the "capitalist roaders" in the Party.[85] In January and February the "rebels" took the ideological offensive and their publications hammered home the now familiar themes: the present form of "class struggle" was primarily a political one directed not at "old" class enemies but at "new bourgeois elements" and new "privileged strata." High cadres' children were singled out as one manifestation of

---

85. "Carry through the Great Proletarian Cultural Revolution to the end," *Hung-ch'i* editorial, No.1, January 1967, in *SCMM* No.558, p.4.

the new system of privilege and they were tarred with the brush of the "United Action Committee" which was denounced as "counter-revolutionary." "Blood pedigree theory" was thus regarded as an ideological rationalisation for an illegitimate elite.

It was in this ideological climate that "origin theory" came to public prominence, arguing the thesis that class origin was of negligible importance in assessing a young person's political quality (some of its detractors called it "no origin theory"). The article setting forth the arguments of "origin theory" was allegedly drafted initially in July 1966, redrafted in September and revised in November 1966. One Peking critic noted that, when he visited Tientsin, Wuhan and Canton in October 1966, he found the imprint of "origin theory" everywhere he went. In February 1967, the article was printed in full in a Peking "rebel" newspaper which sparked off a lively debate, allegedly encouraged by Ch'en Po-ta, during the period from February to early April 1967.

Since the article "Origin Theory" is of considerable intrinsic interest, I have provided a verbatim translation in an appendix in addition to summarising its main arguments here. The editors of the *Middle School Cultural Revolution Bulletin*, which printed the article, saw its publication as a means to counter the continuing influence of "blood pedigree theory" among a large section of middle school Red Guards. The authors of "Origin Theory," the Peking Research Group on the Problem of Family Origin, argued that family origin was a serious social and political problem of long standing. Youths from non-working class families, they maintained, had suffered various forms of discrimination in the years preceding the Cultural Revolution: they could not join the PLA or work on secret projects; their "political treatment" was inferior and their social status was one cut below other people. The situation was all the more serious in view of the large numbers involved: although only about 5 percent of the population were members of the "five [bad] elements," their children were far more numerous. The number was even larger if one took into account the children of capitalists, "elements with unclear histories," "high intellectuals," employees, prosperous middle peasants and middle peasants.

The Research Group divided their response to these problems into three sets of arguments, each supported by select quotations from Chairman Mao. Given the sophistication of their analysis, I shall provide a relatively full precis here:

1. In direct contradiction to the assumptions of "blood pedigree theory," they argued that *the influence exerted on a youth by his social environment far outweighed the influence exerted by his family*. Family influence is only one aspect of the multi-faceted influence of society: there was also the influence of school ("the words of a teacher carry more authority than those of a parent"), friends, the leadership of a person's unit, the mass media, art and culture, social customs and work environment. Since the nature of modern Chinese society is mainly healthy, the prime external influence exerted on youths is therefore beneficial. Given that the relative impact of family socialisation is negligible, moreover, even if the influence of society were bad, this would have the same impact on all youths, whatever their origins. In arguing this point, the Research Group was also contradicting the assumption underlying the official pre-Cultural Revolution "class policy," one apparently shared by Mao himself, that youths of good origins had an automatic advantage in the process of ideological self-transformation. The authors went one step further, arguing that to discuss the relative impact of society and family on young people was to miss the main point. Both of these factors were, after all, "external causes" (*wai-yin*) whereas the decisive factor in personal ideological transformation was the "internal factor" (*nei-yin*) of "subjective initiative." Here, the Research Group was stressing a theme similar to Mao's own views on the power of the individual to transcend environmental constraints through conscious choice and effort.

2. Aiming their criticism squarely at the pre-Cultural "class policy," which they refer to with indirect sarcasm as the position of a "so-called 'fair and just' group," the

Research Group re-emphasised the point that *there is little or no connection between a person's family origin and his political behaviour or reliability*. They based this general point on three arguments. First, members of the same family do not necessarily belong to the same class, an assertion which they supported by citing cases of class enemies who killed their own children because they knew they would betray their parents. Second, the (previous official and Mao Tse-tung's personal) position that both political behaviour *and* family origin should be taken into account was, in the Research Group's view, both unreasonable and impractical. It was unreasonable because it led to a double standard. It was impractical because, in every day practice, it led inevitably to "only looking at family origin, not looking at behaviour" because the criterion of family origin was easier for the basic-level cadre to apply and involved less political risk. Third - and here the Research Group made somewhat sophistical use of Maoist concepts - since good politics and ideology come from struggle, then there is a good case for claiming that youth who are striving to repudiate the bad influence of their family will in fact be more reliable than "hothouse flowers" who grow up in a "red" family environment. To prove the point, they cited the example of the early "five red" Red Guards, particularly organisations of cadres' children such as the United Action Committee, who had followed a "revisionist" line in spite of (or even because of) their excellent family origins.

3. The claims made by youth of "five red" origins in the first phase of the Cultural Revolution that they had suffered social and political discrimination at the hands of P'eng Ch'en's "revisionist clique" were unfounded. In fact, *it was youth of non-"five red" origin who had been discriminated against in a number of areas before the Cultural Revolution*. In the field of college admissions, for example, worker-peasant children had been enrolled preferentially; some colleges totally excluded young people of non-"five red" origins; students from "good" backgrounds received special treatment at college (for example, special classes were arranged to help them study). At the middle school level, they claimed, double

standards operated in the treatment of youth of different origins: for example, reactionary utterances by "five red" youth would tend to be seen as a question of evil external influence, whereas the same indiscretions on the part of "bad" origin youth would be interpreted as an expression of the person's basic class nature; teachers gave special consideration to youth of "good" origin; and League or school-class cadre positions were allocated on the basis of class origin. In factories, moreover, there was discrimination in the selection of "advanced producer" labour models, in the promotion of administrative cadres, in the choice of "masters" to train apprentices or workers to operate "secret" machines, or in recruitment to Red Guard organisations during the Cultural Revolution. In urban neighbourhood units, class origin was taken into account in the election of local residents' committees and in the allocation of jobs to unemployed youth. In the countryside, it was even worse: for example, the children of landlords and rich peasants were excluded from administrative or financial jobs in production teams or brigades and poor and lower-middle peasant youths were preferentially admitted to junior middle schools. In short, the Research Group concluded, youth of "bad" origin in China can be compared to the blacks in the United States, or the "mean people" of Japan. They placed the responsibility squarely on the shoulders of high-ranking "revisionist" cadres who formed a "new privileged stratum" and on the incompetence, laziness and ignorance of basic-level cadres. The article ended with an exhortation to non-"five red" youth to become conscious of their status as a "lower stratum" and to rise up in rebellion to change the situation.

This statement of the major "rebel" position on class origin is remarkable for its breadth and skill of argument. The Research Group appealed effectively to Maoist themes, such as ideological transformation, the importance of struggle and personal initiative, to delineate a position which was clearly at variance with both Mao's own ideas and the official "class policy" before the Cultural Revolution. Many of their arguments were undeniably correct and their claims of alleged discrimination contained a substantial measure of truth. At the same time, their position was an "extreme" one in that it went much further than any of the major "radical" leaders in Peking, including Chiang Ch'ing and Ch'en Po-ta, were willing to go. It was a clear heterodoxy, "radical" in the sense that, if implemented, it would have had profound redistributive implications. It was "egalitarian" in the sense that it demanded equality of opportunity, capsulised in the slogan "In the face of [political] behaviour, all youth are equal." It was based, according to one student admirer from Heilungkiang, on "the central idea that all revolutionary youth of different origins can be equal in the Mao Tse-tung era."[86] It articulated comprehensively the desire of youth from non-"five red" backgrounds, particularly among middle school students, to improve their position in social competition by cancelling out the advantages conferred on "five red" youth by the "class line" and "class policy."

In spite of its wide appeal among educated youth, however, and in spite of its use of Maoist themes, in *political* terms it was on extremely weak ground in the struggle between "conservative" and "rebel" ideas and organisations in early 1967. As the ensuing debate showed, "origin theory" was too vulnerable to "conservative" charges that it was calling for the abolition of classes and class struggle and thus helping the "old" enemies of the revolution and their offspring.

Reactions thus ranged from vitriolic "conservative" hatchet jobs to more sympathetic critiques by independent "rebel" groups. The proponents of "origin theory" accused their opponents of advocating "blood pedigree theory" and labelled them as "counter-revolutionary United Action [Committee] elements."[87] "Conservative" spokesmen, on their side, claimed that "origin theory" had originally been drafted in mid-1966 to undermine the proposed tightening of the "class line" in college admissions and thus defend the interests of non-"five red" youth.[88] Furthermore, the "conservatives"

---

86. *Chung-hsüeh Wen-ko Pao*, February 1967, p.3.
87. "Sentence 'origin theory' to death," *Chiao-kung Chan-pao* [Educational Workers' Combat Bulletin], March 11, 1967.
88. *Ibid.*

alleged the real author was not a middle school student at all but a fifth year college student of bad class origin who was regarded as a "rightist" by his classmates. In fact, urged the "conservatives," the whole purpose of "origin theory" was to give aid and succour to the Party's "old" class enemies. In spite of the fact, for example, that the offspring of the "exploiting classes" had been *over*-represented in the universities before the Cultural Revolution, "origin theory" wanted to extend further the privileges of such youth.[89] "Origin theory" also wanted to infiltrate the offspring of the "bad" classes into positions of leadership under the phoney banner of "equality." If bad class elements or their children were allowed to become officers in the PLA, professors in the universities, cadres in urban neighbourhoods and rural brigades or workers on "secret" projects, continued the "conservatives," China would no longer be a proletarian country.[90] One only had to look at the kind of people who supported "origin theory":

> "Origin theory" certainly has a market... Do you know why people welcome it? I'll tell you. I have seen with my own eyes a fellow jump with joy in front of your leaflet and say: "This time someone's speaking on our behalf!" We grabbed him on the spot and found out he was a rightist.[91]

For the "conservatives," "origin theory" demonstrated clearly the dubious motives and impure class composition of "rebel" organisations. The Research Group had cunningly taken advantage of the campaign against "blood pedigree theory" and in effect turned the "couplet" on its head:

> A dragon produces a bastard; a phoenix produces a turtle; a rat produces a child which flies up to heaven.[92]

---

89. "'Only origin theory' and 'origin theory' are both contrary to Marxism-Leninism and Mao Tse-tung Thought," *Tung Feng Pao* [East Wind Report], March 19, 1967.
90. "Sentence 'origin theory' to death," *loc.cit.*
91. "We oppose whatever the enemy supports," *Chung-hsüeh Wen-ko Pao*, February 1967, p.4.
92. "Bring to light the inferior methods of the 'Peking Research Group on the Problem of Family Origin'," *Tung Feng Pao*, March 19, 1967.

This kind of distortion, argued "conservative" critics, was buttressed by the tendentious use of materials: for example, though the Research Group had mentioned cases of bad class elements who had murdered their own children, they had omitted the fact that, according to Peking police statistics, most young criminals were children of the "five elements."

At the ideological level, the "conservative" critiques maintained, "origin theory" advocated the "revisionist" notion of "the dying away of class struggle" or "the theory of no class differences," a fundamental denial of Mao's theses on the continuation of class struggle in socialist society. The defeated classes still had hopes of restoring their fortunes, particularly in the countryside. Since these "old" class enemies still presented a potential threat, they were bound to have a bad influence on their children. Thus the factor of class origin continued to have considerable significance and to ignore it, as "origin theory" argued, would pose a basic threat to the proletarian power structure:

> We cannot give the children of the exploiting classes equal political rights. If we did this, it would amount to admitting that the older generation of exploiters are all dead and there are no classes in existence any more. This is nothing but the theory of the dying away of class struggle... In the past, power was in our hands and it's still in our hands now! You seven black youth can't wrest it away from us![93]

Finally, "conservative" critics did not accept the social analysis presented by the authors of "Origin Theory."[94] Although willing to admit that youth of "bad" class origin had been victimised in the past, they accused the Research Group of purposely exaggerating this to provide a distorted picture of society dominated by a fascist "privileged elite." This position was a slanderous attack on the socialist system, they maintained, designed to draw people's attention away from the continuing discrimination against youths of "good" class origins.

---

93. "We oppose whatever the enemy supports," *loc.cit.*, p.4.
94. "Promote class analysis, excoriate all forms of absurdity," *Hung-fan Chan-pao* [Red Rebel Combat Bulletin], March 29, 1967, p.4.

In the political and ideological context of the time, the "conservative" critique was an effective one. It highlighted the social heterogeneity of "rebel" groups and their tendency to use ideological arguments to cover sectional interests. Taking a position critical of *both* "origin theory" and "blood pedigree theory," the "conservatives" were thus able to avoid guilt by association with the latter. Their strong reaffirmation of the importance of "old" class categories and class struggle, moreover, produced a strong resonance among urban workers, suburban peasants, youth of "five red" origin and among cadres who felt threatened by the rise of "new" class analysis. Their arguments appeared more "Maoist" than those of the Research Group, moreover, for it was an undeniable fact that Mao himself, and his "radical" associates, still maintained that class origin retained *some* political significance.

The Latter Stages and Aftermath of the Cultural Revolution

The debate over "origin theory" seems to have petered out in April 1967, although I have located one isolated article published later in the year which condemned the Research Group's thesis as a "poisonous weed" and manifestation of a reactionary "reverse current."[95] It seems that the theory was a casualty in the seesaw battle between "rebel" and "conservative" forces which raged throughout 1967 and into 1968. Though it apparently received wide currency and garnered a great deal of support in late 1966 and early 1967, the heyday of "rebel" predominance, its fundamental political and ideological weaknesses seem to have made it something of an embarrassment for the "rebel" side. Whether or not "origin theory" was ever *officially* declared to be "reactionary" or a "poisonous weed" is unclear, but it is clear that, by mid-1967, it had suffered the same fate as "blood pedigree theory": it was ruled to be outside the bounds of legitimate debate. Thus

95. "The reactionary 'theory of social origins' must be criticised," *Great Hue and Cry*, October 2, 1967, trans. in *Chinese Sociology and Anthropology*, Summer 1969, pp.46-48.

the two simple but certain extremes were lopped off, leaving the ambiguous middle. Both "rebels" and "conservatives" continued to joust *within* this middle area and their continuing disagreements were visible in their choice of themes: the "conservatives" stressed educational discrimination against youth of good origin and the continued importance of "old" class enemies, pointed to charges of "impure" elements among the ranks of their opposition and chronicled the evils of P'eng Chen; the "rebels," on the other hand, continued to press home their attack on "revisionist cadres" and their children and on other elements of the new "privileged stratum," stressed the political-ideological definition of class and criticised any overt relapses towards "blood pedigree" type thinking.[96]

Public debate on the issue of class origin declined along with the decline of the Red Guard press in 1968. The leadership in Peking strove to reassert control over the movement and to sort out the confusions resulting from the mass politics of 1966 and 1967. "Conservative" influence grew as former cadres were rehabilitated and combined with PLA representatives and representatives of "conservative" mass organisations within the new revolutionary committees. Resistance from outnumbered "rebels" was increasingly viewed as "bourgeois factionalism;" the original issues of the first stage of the Cultural Revolution, concerning the "class line" in socio-political recruitment, were brought back to the fore; "old" class analysis was reasserted with the beginning of a movement to "purify class ranks" (*ch'ing-li chieh-chi tui-wu*) in early 1968. The primary emphasis in the choice of targets for this movement was placed, as in mid-1966, on the "old" class categories and "historical problems." In "purifying" Party cadres, for example, "capitalist roaders" were provided with the opportunity to redeem themselves, while considerable attention was diverted to search for Kuomintang secret agents and to uncovering treacherous acts committed against the Party

96. For example, see "On the reactionary nature of only position theory (*wei shen-fen lun*)," *Chieh-fang Pao* [Liberation News], March 1968.

before Liberation.[97] Outside the Party, the major targets of the movement were the "old" class enemies, particularly former Kuomintang Party members, military personnel or government officials who still occupied positions of authority or who had remained undetected.[98]

It was in the context of this campaign that an instruction from Chairman Mao was disseminated in May 1968 on the issue of class origin.[99] In this statement, Mao reiterated the major points of the "class policy" in force before the Cultural Revolution: in evaluating young people, class origin and political behaviour were both significant, but the latter was primary and depended on the individual's "class standpoint." This was followed by the announcement of a policy designed specifically to deal with youth of "bad" class origins. They were to be distinguished from their parents and were to be treated as "children who can be educated well."[100]

Although this restatement of the pre-Cultural Revolution "class policy" at the end of the Cultural Revolution implicitly repudiated both of the heterodox "class policies" which emerged during the Cultural Revolution, it did little to dispel the underlying ambiguity of the orthodox "class policy" with its implicit stigma for youth of "bad" background and the problems it presented to basic-level cadres. In the aftermath of the Cultural Revolution, moreover, the "class line" was intensified

---

97. See materials on the movement in *SCMP* Nos.4211, 4212, 4216 and 4220.
98. For example, see *Kuang-chou Hung-tai Hui* [Canton Red Representative Conference], No.9, June 22, 1968, in *SCMP* No.4221, pp.7ff.; *Yi-yüeh Feng-pao* [January Storm News], Canton, No.26, May 1968, in *SCMP* No.4189, esp. p.5.
99. "Chairman Mao's Latest 18-Point Instructions," *Tzu-liao Chuan-chi* [Special Collection of Materials], Canton, May 15, 1968, in *SCMP* No.4201, p.4.
100. For example, see Hung Che-wen, "Chairman Mao's proletarian policies are the life of proletarian political power," *JMJP*, April 20, 1969, in *SCMP* No.4407, p.2; "Peking Hsinhua Printing Plant fully implements Chairman Mao's proletarian policies," *JMJP*, April 24, 1969, in *SCMP* No.4411, p.6; "Implement Chairman Mao's policy and mobilise all active factors," *JMJP*, March 30, 1969, in *SCMP* No.4399, pp.5-7.

in a number of fields to the benefit of youth from worker-peasant backgrounds: for example, in university enrolment, in the administration of primary and middle schools and in Party recruitment. The wider themes of "class struggle" continued to be dominant ideologically and the "natural colour of the labouring people" still remained an inherent political advantage.[101] Thus it seems that many basic-level cadres have continued to "prefer left to right" in implementing the "class policy" and many youth of "bad" family origins have continued to carry an "ideological burden." These problems have cropped up, for example, in the campaign to mobilise urban youth to the countryside to work as peasants. A report in late 1971 pointed to a "leftist" deviation in cadre implementation of the "class policy" (referred to as "only origin theory") resulting from the cadres' apprehension that they would be accused of "confusing the class line" if they treated youth of "bad" origins too well.[102] Another report in late 1972 concerning youth in the PLA Production and Construction Corps in Inner Mongolia pointed to cadre attitudes as the key obstacle to correct policy implementation:

> There are some cadres who admit verbally that ["bad" origin] youths can be educated well - but they feel deep in their hearts that the family influence on these people is great, the class stamp on them is deep and it is difficult for them to transform their ideology.[103]

Though the official policy offers redemption to such youth and criticises such "leftist" deviations, the task of ideological transformation is clearly considered more arduous than for their "five red" compatriots. Given the continuing ideological emphasis on the virtue of the "good" classes, moreover, one might expect that tendencies towards "natural redness" are still strong. Thus, many of the differences in attitude and

---

101. For example, see Shen Tzu-ch'eng, "The natural colour of the labouring people must never fade," *JMJP*, July 25, 1969, in *SCMP* No.4471, pp.9-11.
102. *JMJP*, December 6, 1972.
103. *JMJP*, October 8, 1972.

interest which found expression in Red Guard politics and the debate over "class policy" during 1966 and 1967 still remain as problems for the current leadership to handle or as fuel for a future Cultural Revolution.

CONCLUSION

On questions of "class" and "class origin," therefore, the Cultural Revolution had the impact of dramatising the issues, clarifying the alternatives and creating a new synthesis which did not resolve the underlying problems. First, considerable *ideological diversity* remains at all levels on the definition of "class," notably on the amount of political significance attributed to "old" class categories and the extent to which "new" class analysis has been accepted. At the aggregate level, therefore, the definition of "class" continues to be an ambiguous mixture of "old" and "new" concepts. Second, Chinese society is still characterised by considerable *sociological complexity*. It contains elements of the "old" class system in the form of *ch'eng-fen* and "class origin" categories, and a continuing system of political, social and economic inequalities, which at least in the eyes of "radical" theorists and activists, continue to be fertile soil for the growth of "new bourgeoisie." This latter aspect was clear, for example, in the campaign to discuss "the dictatorship of the proletariat" and "bourgeois right," spearheaded by arch "radicals" Yao Wen-yüan and Chang Ch'un-ch'iao in 1975.[104] Third, the continuing ambiguity over "class" reflects the *political compromise* arising from the Cultural Revolution. During the Cultural Revolution, different definitions of class became linked with opposing political forces and came to reflect radically different conceptions of the purposes of the movement. The "conservatives" wished to restrict the movement to a relatively small-scale purge of errant cadres, to discipline ideological deviance from non-Party sources and to "clean up" the complex socio-political structure of the cities, seen mainly in terms of "old" class categories and political labels. The "radicals," on the other hand, kept on changing the rules of the game at key junctures

---

104. Yao Wen-yüan, "On the social basis of the Lin Piao anti-Party clique," *Peking Review*, March 7, 1975, pp.5-10; Chang Ch'un-ch'iao, "On exercising all-round dictatorship over the bourgeoisie," *Peking Review*, April 4, 1975, pp.5-11.

in an attempt to extend the political scope of the movement and deepen its ideological significance. For them, the movement centred on questions arising from the structure of the new socialist society, questions of the evolving "new" class system. Though these conflicting emphases and political tendencies were brought into uneasy synthesis at the end of the Cultural Revolution, the competition between them continued into the 1970's. Although the institutional and structural changes implied by the "radical" critique were only partly implemented after the Cultural Revolution and although some of its major exponents have been removed from power (notably the May 16th Group, Lin Piao and Ch'en Po-ta), the "radical" position draws its ideological inspiration from Mao himself and continues to provide a potential challenge to any attempt to reinstitutionalise the "revisionist" practices perceived as current before the Cultural Revolution. As the Cultural Revolution showed, however, any concerted effort to translate the "radical" analysis into policy would threaten the positions of substantial sections of the Party elite and thus encounter strong resistance.

At a deeper level of political analysis, however, the findings of this study lead to dissatisfaction with the use of polarised terminology to describe the opposing forces active during the Cultural Revolution. The complexity of the conflict over class related issues and the wide range of distributive issues and policy positions it included highlights the inadequacy of general labels such as "radicals" and "conservatives," "Maoists" and "revisionists," and the political uniformity often attributed to these opposing groups. The label "revisionist," as used by radical "Maoists" during the movement, makes sense when related to two sets of distributive issues. There was a clear tendency among cadres before the Cultural Revolution to interpret the "old" class line in such a way that it brought about redistribution in favour of themselves and their families (for example, favouring their children through the honorific labels "revolutionary cadre" and "revolutionary soldier"). At the same time, however, the more technocratic emphases of alleged "revisionists" within the Party leadership led them to adopt more liberal class policies towards skilled strata, notably old intelligentsia, in view of their potential contribution to national development. On the other hand, it is equally clear that there were significant differences among "revisionist" cadres on the political significance of the "old" class line. Leaders such as P'eng Chen, for example, apparently regarded class status or origin as relatively unimportant while others such as T'ao Chu or T'an Ch'en-lin took a "harder" line on the issue. It would thus be a mistake to argue that the label "revisionist" necessarily implied an abandonment or downplaying of the original redistributive aims of the CCP.

Turning to the "radicals" or "Maoists," moreover, these labels also conceal a variety of positions on class related issues. There is coherence in the sense that various radical groups used the language of class in a redistributive way to attack the various privileges arrogated before the Cultural Revolution by ranking cadres and other privileged groups, notably the urban intelligentsia. But such redistributive class slogans reflected a wide variety of attitudes and interests among the "radicals," ranging from the "pure" ideological positions of those who had fully internalised the ideas of the "new" class struggle to a variety of groups who were using this language to further their own factional or sectional interests. On the issue of the "old" class line, moreover, the "radical" camp was very heterogeneous: many radicals berated "revisionist" cadres for betraying the redistributive goals implicit in the "old" class line but others, such as the groups supporting "origin theory," elaborated a "radical" position which in effect *did away with* the policy of redistribution on the basis of class origins. Thus the simplicity of ideological class categories overlaid a highly complex system of distributive issues and political motivations which illustrates the dangers implicit in attempting to deduce political alignments from general ideological labels.

Turning to the future, the fact that ideological differences on the nature of class are related to a complex system of social interests and political forces implies that a major change in the official definition of "class," even if technically possible, would be politically unfeasible in the near future. Class categories, both "old" and "new," have sunk deep roots in Chinese society, creating enduring sets of beliefs, interests and political attachments which are difficult to rearrange by definitional fiat (such as, for example, a major redefinition of *ch'eng-fen* categories or the complete abolition of the "old" *ch'eng-fen* categories). One might hypothesise, however, that, as that generation who were given *ch'eng-fen* in the early 1950's grow old and die off, the political significance of "old" *ch'eng-fen* categories will gradually decline and they will be replaced by categories appropriate to the new society (for example, "commune member" (*she-yüan*) rather than "poor peasant" or "middle peasant"). Thus the focus of "class" politics would be more and more unambiguously concerned with the structure of the *new* socialist society. The extent to which the "new" class analysis takes root and prevents the evolution of Chinese society into a system of entrenched inequality depends a great deal on the extent to which "radical" Maoism retains its political influence within the Chinese leadership.

In our case study of the debate over "class policy" during the Cultural Revolution, we examined in detail the political impact of ambiguous ideological definitions of class when they were embodied in concrete policies. For the younger generation of China they were translated into two principles of distributive justice, institutionalised in the "class policy," which had different implications for the socio-political opportunities available to different groups. One principle, "pay attention to [class or family] origin," reflected a redistributive revolutionary egalitarian ideal, stressing positive discrimination in favour of previously underprivileged sectors of the population. The other principle, "put the primary stress on [political] behaviour," reflected the "new" behavioural definition of "class" which offered a universalistic standard for *all* Chinese youths, regardless of their class origins. The inherent ambiguity of this policy, its fluctuating interpretations and the frequent gap between policy and practical implementation created constellations of conflicting attitudes towards the nature of "class" and different positions on the issues arising from the "class policy" among Chinese youth. These differences were expressed in their full complexity during the Cultural Revolution when the ideological diversity on this issue gave rise to two heterodoxies, "blood pedigree theory" and "origin theory." This very diversity, however, necessitated compromise which took the form of a reiteration of the ambiguous "class policy" prevalent before the Cultural Revolution. Though the official "class policy" was not changed, the Cultural Revolution did bring changes in three related areas: first, the privileges of cadres' children seem to have been restricted though not abolished; second, since the "class line" in recruitment to universities has been strengthened after the Cultural Revolution, this makes it more difficult for youth who are not of worker-peasant origin to gain access to higher education; and third, since the importance of examinations has declined as a criterion for educational advancement and much of the power to make decisions over young people's futures has been transferred from the schools to basic-level units, factories and rural production brigades, this removes one of the advantages available for youth of non-working class origin before the Cultural Revolution and leaves their future more in the hands of overwhelmingly worker-peasant basic-level cadres in production units. In the short term, therefore, the position of non-working class youth seems to have become more difficult. In the longer term, however, as the passage of time brings yet another generation whose "origin" depends on their parents' position in the new socialist society and not the "old society," the issue of class origin may well lose its political force or, if translated purely into "new" class terms, become a weapon used by "radicals" to prevent the inter-generational transmission of privilege and the formation of permanently disadvantaged groups.

In summary, these sets of "class" issues illustrate the tensions, ambiguities and contradictions which make Chinese politics so difficult to comprehend and so fascinating to analyse. They testify to the extent to which ideological categories have restructured society and penetrated into the consciousness of the people, creating new conceptions of society and a new political language with its own internal disputes and disagreements. Finally, it hopefully illustrates the process whereby ideology, policy, power and interest become intertwined in a complex political process which outsiders were able to glimpse for a while in its full richness during the Cultural Revolution.

APPENDIX

Chung-hsüeh Wen-ko Pao [Middle School Cultural Revolution News] Special Issue, February 1967.

(Published by the Propaganda Department of the Middle School Students Revolutionary Rebel Headquarters.)

"Origin Theory" (*Ch'u-shen Lun*)

The Peking Research Group on the Problem of Family Origin

[The article is prefaced by editorial comments in fine print, much of which was blurred and unreadable. Therefore only a paraphrase of the introductory section is provided. The article itself is translated verbatim.]

[Editorial comment: In spite of the efforts of the rebel faction, the mass movement in Peking's middle schools is still not in full swing. The main obstruction is the continuing influence of the reactionary theory of only [stressing class] origin (*wei ch'u-shen lun*). Advocates of this theory are trying to split the student body into grades and create a new privileged stratum. This leads to feelings of "natural redness" (*tzu-lai hung*) on the part of the children of revolutionary parents and an inferiority complex and pessimism on the part of others. The theory must be smashed!

We hail the appearance of this article since it demonstrates the bankruptcy of "only origin theory." Of course, some people think it's a poisonous weed, but Chairman Mao teaches us that, in history, new and correct things do not gain majority recognition at first and only develop and gain acceptance through struggle.]

The problem of family origins is a serious social problem of long standing.

This problem covers a wide area. If we estimate landlord, rich peasant, counter-revolutionary, bad and rightist elements to be 5 percent of the country's population, their children and close relations will be several times that number (and we are not counting the children of capitalists, elements with unclear histories (*li-shih pu-ch'ing-pai fen-tzu*) and high intellectuals, still less the children of the employee, prosperous middle peasant (*fu-yü chung-nung*) and middle peasant strata). It is easy to imagine that the number of young people who are not of five red (*hung wu lei*) origins is large indeed. Since China is a backward country, there were only 2,000,000 industrial workers before liberation. As a result there are very few youth from really proletarian family backgrounds. This large group of young people whose [family] origin is not good cannot, in general, join the armed forces and they cannot work on secret projects. As a result, if we look concretely at individual units, people of non-five red origins constitute the absolute majority.

Because of the influence of a reactionary line which is 'left' in form but right in essence, they have often been unable to enjoy equal political treatment, particularly those youths from so-called "seven black" (*hei ch'i lei*) origins, those "sons of bitches" who have already become objects of dictatorship. They are seen as "criminals" by birth. Under the influence of this line, origin is used to decide nearly everything. Youths whose origins are not good are one cut below everybody, even to the point of being deprived of their rights to repudiate their [reactionary] families, to defend the Party centre and Chairman Mao and to join the Red Guards. At this time, there are many innocent youths who are dying a premature death, drowning in the deep waves of only origin theory. In the face of this kind of serious problem, anyone who cares about the nation's fate cannot but confront and investigate the issue. Those viewpoints which appear dispassionate and universally flexible are really callous and hypocritical. We must use the methods of unmasking and criticism to protect Chairman Mao's revolutionary line. Below, seeking solutions from Chairman Mao's works and from social practice, we convey our viewpoint by dividing the question into three sections:

1. <u>The Problem of Social Influence and Family Influence</u>

Let's begin with a couplet which spread poison far and wide:

When the old man's a hero, the son's a good chap;
When the old man's a reactionary, the son is a bad egg;
This is basically the case.

The process of debating this couplet was actually a process of insulting youths who were not of good origins. In this kind of debate, the best outcome for a person was merely if he could avoid being considered a bad egg, that's all. There were very few in the beginning who dared to offer a refutation. Even if anyone dared, it was often very timidly. Actually the upper half of this couplet was borrowed from the Great Mountain King Tou Erh Tun of feudal times. Surely it doesn't require much guts nowadays to criticise Tou Erh Tun. Other people say that this couplet played a positive role. Is that so? Chairman Mao says: "That which is true serves the people's interests; that which is false does not serve the people's interests." To judge whether the couplet has played a good role or not, we must see whether it is true - i.e. whether it conforms to Mao Tse-tung Thought.

This couplet is not true. It's absolutely false. Its error derives from the assumption that the influence of family is more important than the influence of society. It cannot see that social influence plays the decisive role. In plain terms, it only recognises the father's influence and holds that the father is all important.

Practical experience happens to provide a totally opposite conclusion: social influence far exceeds family influence; family influence is subordinate to social influence.

From the time a child is born he experiences simultaneously these two types of influence. When his intellect develops a little, he enters the big gate of school. The words of the teacher convey more weight than those of his parents; the resonance of collective education is stronger than that of individual tuition; he spends more time at school than at home; the rain and dew of the Party and the bright sunlight of Mao Tse-tung Thought nourish this new born sprout. The influence of society becomes the main factor.

The influence of friends, instruction from the leadership, information in newspapers, books, literature and art, the force of habit, the moulding impact of work environment, etc. - all have an ineradicable influence on a person. We call these collectively "social influence." There is no way for family influence to compete with this.

Even if we take family influence, that too is a part of social influence. One cannot decide the nature of a person's family influence by looking mechanically at his father. If he has a heroic father and a reactionary mother, the [family] influence is not necessarily good. If the parents are both heroes but the children are allowed to run wild, sometimes they turn out even worse. The mother's thought may be good, but if her methods of education are too simple and strict, the effects may also be the opposite of those intended. Similarly, even if the father is bad, it doesn't necessarily mean that the family influence is definitely bad. Lenin is an example of this. In sum, one cannot judge the nature of a person's family influence by mechanical reference to his origin. Origin is merely a piece of reference material for evaluating family influence.

Generally speaking, the influence exerted by our society is good. This is because our social system is incomparably superior, because our Party has consistently emphasised politics and has paid the greatest attention to the growth of the younger generation. The overwhelming majority of our people love the new society. Of course, we cannot neglect the sharp and complex nature of class struggle as well, nor the fact that we still exist in a vast ocean of petty bourgeoisie. Our culture and education system are in need of thorough reform. Sometimes, moreover, the influence of society is not wholly beneficial. Any youth, no matter what his origin, who is subject to continual bad social influence, will generally give in to the bad influence, making this or that kind of mistake. But if he is guided to deal with the problem, he can quickly cast off old things and return to the correct standpoint. Thus to deliberately make young people carry the burdens of their family or their history on their backs is cruel and reflects an incorrect line. Since the influence of society is incomparably strong and yet is not totally beneficial, it is wrong for a youth of *any* origin to abandon the task of remoulding his thought. In transforming one's thought, youths of good origins have no advantage over youths who are not of good origins.

Whether we talk of family influence or social influence, they are both external factors. If we overemphasise the idea of influence, this is an expression of mechanically disregarding the factor of subjective initiative. Men can choose the direction before them. This is because truth is always more powerful and more inspirational. Do you really believe that Marxism-Leninism is incomparably correct? Do you really believe that Mao Tse-tung Thought is an invincible ideological weapon? Do you really recognise that internal [subjective] factors play the decisive role? If you do, then you shouldn't maintain that influence exerted by a father is more powerful than any other. Otherwise, you can only show that your thinking is hopelessly muddled.

2. The Question of Putting Stress on Behaviour (*piao-hsien*)

If you have no arguments against the assertion that the influence of society is greater than the influence of family and if you cannot deny that the beneficial influence of contemporary society is the major factor and if you cannot but agree that [family] origin and family influence have no necessary connection, then we can go on to look into some problems of "put the stress on behaviour."

At the beginning of the Great Proletarian Cultural Revolution, many people said that "put the stress on behaviour" was a revisionist viewpoint. Afterwards, when they heard that it was Chairman Mao who originated the policy, they hurriedly changed their tune. It's clear that they just don't understand this policy. If you make them explain this policy, they can't avoid arbitrary distortion. Confining ourselves to a brief analysis here, we shall examine three types of propositions to see whether or not they conform with Mao Tse-tung Thought.

(*i*) Origin and *Ch'eng-fen* are Totally Different:

Superficially "fair and just" comrades often say this to youth whose origin is not good: "One, we take *ch'eng-fen* into consideration; two, we don't only take *ch'eng-fen* into consideration; three, we put the main stress on political behaviour."[1] This is missing the real point.

Comrade Chiang Ch'ing has explained this expression. She said: "This is spoken of individuals who have turned their back on their own class." What does Comrade Chiang Ch'ing's explanation mean? To take an example, Engels was himself a capitalist, but he turned his back on his class and became a first generation communist citizen and a brilliant leader of the working class. In the Paris Commune, moreover, some of the committeemen were themselves bourgeois elements, but they were publicly recognised representatives of the working class. We had this kind of people during our own country's revolution. Can we erase their historical achievements because their *ch'eng-fen* was bad? No! We must stress political behaviour. This is called "not putting exclusive stress on *ch'eng-fen*." We think that this principle also applies to the opposite situation. If a person of miner *ch'eng-fen* betrays the proletariat and the revolution, we must also put the main stress on political behaviour. There is no reason at all to restrain our anger at his crimes. To put the matter in a nutshell, Li Su-ming was a landlord element, but he made the good suggestion of "less troops, simpler administration" to the border region government. Chairman Mao praised him, saying: "No matter what kind of person you are...if the methods you propose are beneficial to the people, then we will act as you say." This implies that we should not let the identity of a man obscure what he says and it is another example of not laying exclusive stress on *ch'eng-fen*.

Origin and *ch'eng-fen* are two totally different things. The father's *ch'eng-fen* is the son's origin. It is correct to talk of the family in feudal society as being a social unit with

---

1. When "Origin Theory" was published, we had to phrase it this way. Now we have seen that "the people who appear just and fair" - Li Hsüeh-feng, who said this in a speech to the Ninth Plenum of the Youth League Central Committee in July 1966, and people like him - have now become representatives of the bourgeois reactionary line.

the son inheriting his father's position. But, with the advent of capitalist society, this was no longer wholly correct. Family ties had already been loosened and the younger generation had already been integrated into society. When we get to socialist society, however, most children and youth receive proletarian education and are prepared to serve or already are serving the cause of the proletariat. If we still view the father and son as identical, then we'll be "out of step with present trends."

In 1939, Chairman Mao stated in "The Chinese Revolution and the Chinese Communist Party" that the intellectuals of that time belonged to the petty bourgeoisie. He did not make distinctions and assign intellectuals of different class origins to different categories.

Chairman Mao again pointed out in 1957 in "On the Correct Handling of Contradictions among the People": "Although many of our university students do not come from labouring class families, yet, apart from a small minority, they are all patriotic and support socialism...." This is another case to prove the point.

Thus we can see that members of the same family are clearly not members of the same class. Even class enemies are clear on this point. For example, during a [political] movement, a middle-level people's court in Peking reported in a verdict that a counter-revolutionary rich peasant element took a weapon to his three sons and hacked them to death in the night because they had reported him. Again, according to a leaflet, the secretary of a commune factory in the city - a degenerate turncoat element - drowned his own child with his own hands before committing suicide. In his will he said that, if his son had grown up, he would not have sought revenge for him.

Origin and *ch'eng-fen* cannot be treated as equal. There is a bit of dialogue which is worth your attention: A: (a student) "What origin are you?;" B: "What about you?;" A: "I'm a five red; my father's a worker;" B: "Well I'm well ahead of you. I *am* a worker."

If we regard only *ch'eng-fen* theory as unreasonable, how is it that only origin theory is still with us?

Some people make use of Chairman Mao's words to refute us, saying: "In a class society, every person lives in a fixed class status and different types of thinking cannot but impress different class stamps." This is 100 percent correct. Landlords and capitalists who have lived for a long time as members of an exploiting class must bear the ideological imprint of their class. As a result, if they want to become a person again, they must change themselves radically - this is the basis of our [policy of] "pay attention to *ch'eng-fen*." But one cannot view their children in the same way. Particularly in the case of youths who have grown up in the new society, can we say that they have lived as members of an exploiting class? Where on earth is there an exploiting class that has not exploited? There's no such thing. It is not merely the family which leaves an ideological imprint on a person but, more importantly, the society. Our society of today is a great school of Mao Tse-tung Thought. The class status of youth is either that of a labourer or on the way to becoming a labourer. To continue to describe them in terms of "*ch'eng-fen*" is to drive them into the realm of antagonistic classes.

We must draw a clear and unmistakable line between origin and *ch'eng-fen*. Anyone who erases this dividing line, however "left" he might appear, is in reality effacing a class boundary.

(*ii*) <u>There is Little Connection between Origin and Behaviour</u>:

Comrades on the "fair and just" side don't talk about *ch'eng-fen*. "We look at origin," they say, "and we also look at [political] behaviour." This is a reprint of "the theory that origin equals *ch'eng-fen*." If we compare the two, it's a case of a lesser and greater evil. There's not much difference between them. Origin is dead, behaviour is living. If we use a dead and a live standard simultaneously to evaluate a person, can we reach the same conclusion? We've already analysed this in the first question raised by our article: origin is one determinant of family influence and family influence is one determinant of behaviour, but only a subsidiary one. The main factor in determining behaviour is social influence. As a result, origin and behaviour are not identical in any way. One can only find out whether a person has been subject to good or bad influence from practice. By practice we mean a person's political behaviour. If he behaves well, then the influence was good; if he behaves badly, then the influence was bad. This has no connection at all with origin.

Putting the matter in context, if we must take into account both origin and behaviour, then we may ask the following: if a person's origin is not good and his behaviour is good, does that mean we can wipe out his achievements? If his origin is good and his behaviour is bad, does that mean we can gloss over a person's defects? If his origin is bad and his behaviour bad also, does that mean we should make his crime one notch more serious? If his origin and behaviour are both good, does that mean we should exaggerate a person's merits? Surely this kind of action is unreasonable.

"Look at origin and look at behaviour also" in reality cannot avoid slipping into the mire of "only look at origin, don't look at behaviour." It's very easy to check on origin. One flip of the file, the problem's solved and all's well. Alternatively you can meet a person on the street, ask him "What origin are you?" and thereby know everything about him. It's really simple and convenient. Checking a person's [political] behaviour is rather bothersome, particularly for that impossible group of doubters who don't believe either your everyday behaviour or your behaviour in times of turmoil; who doubt both your past and your present behaviour and even prepare to doubt your future behaviour; who doubt until you die and only then, when the coffin lid is closed, give a final verdict. Finally even they feel that they've been too suspicious. What if you look at origin? You can solve a big problem in two seconds. Some people, moreover, have no fixed criteria for evaluating behaviour. People who like being buttered up regard flattery as the best form of behaviour. People who like fake humility regard the *kow-tow* as the best form of behaviour.

People who cling to an erroneous line think that perpetual repentance on the part of youths of bad origins is the best kind of behaviour. What can compare with origin? All you need is "if the old man's a hero, the son's a good chap; if the old man's a reactionary, the son's a bad egg; if the old man's just average, the son's a fence-sitter" - just three phrases and your problem's solved.

Let's see what Chairman Mao taught us. Chairman Mao said: "To distinguish finally between revolutionary, non-revolutionary and counter-revolutionary intellectuals, one must see whether or not they are willing, in mind and action, to unite with the worker-peasant masses. We are proposing a standard here. I consider it the only standard." Is this one and only standard that of origin?

Chairman Mao also said: "Any person who stands on the side of the revolutionary people belongs to the revolutionary side...." Did he mention origin here?

Do the five conditions for revolutionary successors proposed by Chairman Mao include origin as a condition?

Point 15 of the Sixteen Points firmly implements the Party's class line and discusses whom to rely on, whom to unite with and whom to oppose. Is this based on origin?

Is there any mention of origin as a criterion among the three criteria for joining the revolutionary left? None at all! What connection is there between the question of whether a person has a good or bad origin and whether he is revolutionary or not? Even if his origin is not good, he can still join the revolutionary left, and become a successor to the revolutionary cause and a bulwark element of the revolution.[2] In the face of

---

2. Soon after "Origin Theory" was posted up, the space beside these words was filled with phrases such as "great poisonous weed," "nonsense" and the like, venting the cheap outrage of T'an Li-fu and his ilk. They were pretty smart because this is the essential part of "Origin Theory." Nevertheless, history is impartial. Today, a large number of Red Guards are taking this statement as part of their organisational programme. One Red Guard organisation has written: "In the past only so-called "five reds" could join Red Guard organisations. This does not conform to Mao Tse-tung Thought so we oppose it." We convey revolutionary respects to these organisations for their brave conduct.

performance, all youths are equal. Youths who are not of good origins don't need to be granted their place in the revolution through the generosity of others, they cannot be kept behind the sidelines. Who constitutes the backbone? This can't be decided in the fetus. We do not recognise any right that cannot be attained through individual effort. The most determined revolutionaries are those who behave the most superbly. Nobody can say that Wang Chieh's glory was below that of Lei Feng.

Talking of how to view [political] behaviour reminds us of a story by an ancient thinker. He said that very fast horses were a common occurrence but experts who understood fast horses were few and far between. Usually when people examine a horse, they judge its quality by its mother, its external appearance, the area where it was bred or its price. Unfortunately they forget to try the horse out by letting it gallop to see if it can in fact run fast. This way, they cannot tell which horse is a very fast one. Aren't some people today just like that? They only consider dead materials such as origin or social relations and forget altogether the true basis of evaluation, [political] behaviour. Over a long period, this has not only spoiled the fast horses, but has turned even ordinary horses into "sons of bitches."

We must put origin and behaviour in their proper perspective. Origin is no criterion for judging whether or not a youth is revolutionary. The only standard is behaviour. The broad majority of youth with both good origin and good behaviour should not oppose this statement. If you really think good origin means good behaviour, then you may have outdone the behaviour of youths from bad origins as well. It is only those with awful behaviour who raise the great banner of origin and use it as a tiger skin; they take their father as their trademark and expect others to appreciate them. We say this: if you behave badly, for example, by stubbornly sticking to a reactionary line or by not studying and using Chairman Mao's works, etc., then the fact that your origin is one of the first three of the five reds (revolutionary cadre, revolutionary armyman, revolutionary martyr) won't help you at all.

Things such as origin or social relations can only count as reference materials. But if we want to gain a clear understanding of a youth's political behaviour, then these two factors don't even have reference value.

(*iii*) Origin and Reliability Have Nothing in Common:

Comrades of the "just and fair" group have changed their tune this time: "Of course, the children of the five black elements are not entirely the same as their parents...." Reading between the lines, they mean that they are of course not the same as five red children. Why? Because "they are not reliable" (this time they use utilitarianism as their magic charm).

But why are they not reliable? "In one way or another, they have been subject to bad influence!" say the proponents of the theory that external factors are decisive. But they don't mention that a bad family origin doesn't necessarily mean a bad influence, or that family influence is subordinate to the influence of society. Well, is it true that, if a person's family influence is rather bad but the influence of society is good, his behaviour will be rather bad as well? This is not a qeustion of an algebraic but a dialectical relationship. Chairman Mao says: "There is no construction without destruction." He adds: "When destruction comes to the fore, the seeds of construction lie within it." If one doesn't struggle with non-proletarian thoughts in one's own brain, how can proletarian thought be firmly established? We often describe those youths who have only undergone red education without experiencing a testing process of ideological transformation as hothouse flowers. They can't stand stress and pressure, they are quick to waver and change their position and are an easy prey for evil men. Isn't that so? Take those good chaps of rather enviable origin who advocated "If the old man's a hero, the son's a good chap" at the beginning of the Great Cultural Revolution. Didn't they carry out a revisionist line afterwards and become spokesmen for the bourgeoisie? Were they "reliable"? The origins of those great teachers and leaders of the great revolutionary cause of the proletariat,

Marx, Lenin and Chairman Mao, were all bad. This reality is certainly not accidental. The crux of the problem lies not in origin, but in ideological transformation.

People who are heavily affected by the family concept claim that "the children of revolutionary cadres have no thought of restoration; they could not revolt against their fathers." Often, restoration is brought about without people being aware of it. The powerholders in the party taking the capitalist road who have been uncovered in this movement and the people they have promoted over the past few years are generally of good origin. Have they been reliable? Afterwards came the work teams, 'left' in form but right in essence, which publicly decreed or secretly promoted policies which discriminated against youths who were not of good origin. Those elected to revolutionary committees at that time were mostly of good origin. As a result, they mostly became promoters of the work teams' reactionary line. Were they reliable? A certain responsible person of the Peking Middle Schools Red Guards had two secretaries, one male and one female, and a chauffeur. On top of this, he had a small car, a motor-bike, a watch, a camera, a tape recorder, etc. Comrade Ch'en Po-ta called him a phoney Red Guard. It is clear that the danger of restoration cannot be removed by sole reliance on people of good origin. In ancient times there was an empress called Wu Tze-t'ien who put to death the great official Shang-kuan Yi but made the official's daughter stay as her personal secretary. Some people were concerned for her safety. She replied: "All you need is good administration and people will naturally become contented and faithful. So why the fuss?" Look at those who pushed the reactionary line: they fear Mao Tse-tung Thought and have failed to carry out the Party's policies. How can they be considered revolutionary youth? Ridiculous! They are more myopic than even a feudal empress on this point and yet they call themselves "proletarian warriors!" Our great leader Chairman Mao would never have included origin among his conditions for successors. Under his leadership, youths are the most reliable since his policies are the most correct and his lines are the most clear. Otherwise, even if all young people have good origins, as in the Soviet Union where the exploiting classes were expelled after the victory of the revolution, the situation is still not secure.

A lot of people advocate the theory of reliability, but they have no decent arguments. Could this be the "class viewpoint"? Nothing like it! This is "class prejudice." It has nothing to do with the proletariat and is pretty close to the petty bourgeoisie. These people have not established the idea of "public" in their minds. Their consciousness is permeated with selfishness, so when they evaluate themselves and others, they cannot avoid distortion. According to their viewpoint, if the old man is reactionary, the son's a bad egg. But if the sons continue to be bad eggs for generation after generation, then mankind can never be liberated, communism can never succeed. So these people are not communists. In their view, the son takes after his father and they are unaware that human thought comes from practice. So they are not materialists. In their view, if a person's mother and father are good, then his thought is certain to be good, without need for tough ideological transformation and ideological struggle. Thus, they are not revolutionaries. They are not revolutionary themselves and they won't allow youths whose origin is not good to become revolutionary. They dub themselves "naturally red" but who would have thought that their "natural redness" is nothing more than filling for stale mooncakes.[3]

We must trust the broad masses of youth brought up under Mao Tse-tung Thought, first and foremost those with good political behaviour. We cannot use a traditional theory to demean one section of men and elevate another. This is an inferior type of political method which is completely unreasonable. We will not allow bourgeois class prejudice to replace the proletarian class viewpoint. Of course any youth with prospects ought to resolve to remould himself. In this way, even if he is subject to evil influences, he can change bad things into good and obstacles into advantages....

---

3. "Natural redness" is the name given to a type of mooncake in Peking.

3. The Question of Victimisation

In 1961 a certain leader* remarked as follows: "There should be no uncrossable chasm between youths of different origins."

It shouldn't exist, but unfortunately it does. What has caused it?

Remember the first stage of this movement. The problem of victimisation was raised first by some trendy individuals. After that, everybody was saying that they'd suffered at the hands of the revisionist clique. The revisionist clique was so reactionary that one could hardly count as a revolutionary if one had not only not been victimised but on the contrary had received favours from them. Thus even T'an Li-fu said he'd been victimised. Economic victimisation? During the period of hardship, he feasted on Dutch condensed milk. Political victimisation? With a mind as reactionary as his, he still got into the Party. How could he resemble a young gentleman who has suffered injustice? The newly reorganised *Peking Daily* gave a great deal of space to articles on the complaints of five red origin youth. They said they were victims of the revisionist line carried out by the former municipal committee. It should be pointed out that *all* young people were victimised. Why just mention youth of good origin? Let us look at what they suffered.

1. "The university refused to admit us but threw its doors open wide to exploiting class children;" 2. "In universities, youths from good origins were scorned by the professor when their work was bad;" 3. "Some youths of bad origins were actually made cadres;" 4. "etc...." If this is what they mean by victimisation, then the victims are clearly youths of *bad* origins. A large newspaper in our august capital confused right and wrong to such an extent that it is no wonder it died a natural death! Let the facts speak for themselves!

---

*The Research Group is referring here to Foreign Minister Ch'en Yi who made this comment in a major 1961 policy statement. By the time this pamphlet appeared, however, Ch'en was under heavy Red Guard attack and this probably accounts for the failure to cite him by name. See above, p.12.

If we think back to the period when the revisionist clique was in power, when university student enrolment was completed each year, the former Ministry of Higher Education always used to make a public announcement: "This year we are enrolling a large number of worker-peasant and revolutionary cadres' children preferentially." Quite a number of universities almost completely excluded children of the five blacks. As for the important departments within the university, there was no possibility of entering them. Schools thus took pride in establishing "worker-peasant-revolutionary cadre classes." Was this "throwing school doors wide open to exploiting class children"? The students of good origin got special treatment after they'd enrolled. A lot of universities set up organisations similar to "poor and lower-middle peasant associations" alongside the [Young Communist] League. Ever since this movement started, people have prevented seven black children from going on journeys to link up with other youth (*ch'uan-lien*), they have used origin as a weapon to attack fellow students who dared to write big character posters, they have prevented youths whose origins were not good from joining all sorts of struggle organisations, and they have used [the theme of family] origin to incite one section of the masses against another. Nobody finds this surprising. It is clear that victimisation of youth from bad origins is a common event. As for the claim that the academic work of youths of five red origin is poor, this is purely an insult to them. Why should one think that origin and study are in definite contradiction? It's the same situation in the middle schools. According to materials on research into disorderly school classes published by the former Peking Municipal Education Office, an investigation of students who "caused disturbances" showed that most of them had very good origins. (N.B.: "Causing disturbances" has nothing to do with making rebellion. The report talks mostly of sexual promiscuity and theft.) The students in disorderly classes who kept quiet while the rest made a noise tended to be of pretty bad origin. If asked why they kept quiet, the reply would be: "My origin's bad. If others make trouble, they don't get into hot water. If I make a row, I'm in trouble." This is no lie and it applies to primary as well as middle schools. There's one case of a school principal who told his young teachers. "If two children say something reactionary at the same time, for the youth of good origin it's a matter of [external] influence, for the youth of bad origin it's a matter of their nature." Once all the Young Pioneer cadres of bad origins in certain schools were voted out - I don't know whether this was a response to a directive by the former city Youth League committee or not. In the past few years, all middle school League and class cadres have been examined from the point of view of origin. Most teachers have paid special attention to youths of good origin (especially the children of revolutionary cadres), perhaps under the influence of public opinion, or perhaps as an expression of their own feelings. They've always treated youths of good origin specially (particularly children of revolutionary cadres). The opposite phenomenon is purely exceptional. If it weren't, then teachers would soon get accused of "having no class viewpoint."

This kind of phenomenon has been very common in factories. Almost all the administrative cadres promoted over the past three or four years have been from good origins. On the list of candidates for advanced worker positions, there's a column dealing with origin. Some factories have the regulation that master workers of bad origins may not take on apprentices or may not handle secret machine tools. At the beginning of this movement, it was also laid down that "workers from bad origins have the right to vote but cannot be candidates." When the crimes committed by the powerholders in each factory were summarised, the phenomenon of so-called "calling for surrender" (i.e. promoting a certain person of bad origin to be a technical cadre) was a very important factor. One can be certain that future cliques in authority would not risk doing this again! When the factories organised Red Guards, moreover, the limitations on origin were very strict. If we search through central documents, we can only find the instructions to rely on workers. We haven't come across an instruction to the effect that we should rely on workers of good origin only. Who split workers into two factions?

There are a lot of these examples in the countryside. In places where the representatives of revisionism carried out the "four cleans [movement]," they [arbitrarily] classified *ch'eng-fen* for the children of landlords and rich peasants. If they behaved badly, their origin was made into their *ch'eng-fen*; if their behaviour was average, they became "agricultural labourers" (*nung-yeh lao-tung-che*); if their behaviour was good, they were classified as "middle peasants." Why were those who behaved well made into middle peasants? Couldn't they be counted as poor and lower-middle peasants? If poor and lower-middle peasant children behave badly, should we likewise classify them as landlords or rich peasants? Is [political] behaviour the result of origin or is origin the result of behaviour? If your origin is not good, then you can't get all sorts of administrative, financial or managerial jobs and you can't move outside your village. In rural areas without universal education, a person needs three recommendations to get to junior middle school - from a teacher, from the poor and lower-middle peasant association and from the head of the brigade. Of course, are any of these willing to support children of bad origin? The brigade head says in his introduction: "This kid has a good origin, he's obedient and hard working. Let's send him!" This is how people get into junior middle school.[4]

It's a similar situation in other sectors of society. In elections for residents' committees in Peking's streets over the past two years, origin has been a major qualification for candidacy. There's even a section for origin on the employment registration form for unemployed youth printed by the street office. On the employment form, there are two important sections - besides the one for origin, there is one for a brief personal history. All the people who write their brief personal histories are young, so naturally their situations are pretty

---

4. In some rural areas there was a rule to the effect that, in the transition from primary to junior-middle school, origin should count for 60 percent, behaviour for 20 percent, academic accomplishment 5 percent, other factors 15 percent.

much the same. When the employing units come to choose workers, they always choose those of good origin. Otherwise, if they ignore youths of good origin and only take those of bad origin, what kind of thought would this reflect? Thus, youths who don't get into schools and are seeking work at the neighbourhood level pile up year by year and most of them are from bad origins. They only get the chance of being allocated to a job when there's a glut of jobs available for allocation.[5]

"Origin oppresses people to death" is completely right. If you're a person who has overcome his "class prejudice," you can provide a greater number of typical examples than us. Who, then, has been victimised? If things continue to develop like this, how will they differ from the caste system of the blacks in the United States, the untouchables in India and the mean people in Japan?

"This is a test for them!" Away with your test! You evaluate everybody as pretty much the same as their fathers, i.e. they want restoration, they're not reliable, they're too backward. On the other hand, you make such heavy demands on people and think they can bear this impossible type of test. What a contradiction between your evaluations and your demands! Have you forgotten Marx's words? "It is very immoral to demand that unfortunates become perfect."

"Their fathers oppressed our fathers, so we're not polite to them now!" What a narrow pedigree viewpoint! In a capitalist society, if a father goes bankrupt, all the son has to do to sever relations with him is to make an announcement renouncing his right of inheritance. Who would have thought

---

5. We suggest that comrades interested in pursuing this question should do some social research. You can investigate how many people in your own unit are of good origin. How many of bad origin? What percentage have administrative jobs? What percentage are Party or Youth League members? Are there any cases where people have been excluded from political activities because their origin was bad? Apart from this, you could examine periodicals like *China Youth* from 1964 on. Comrades will find articles in these revisionist controlled publications expressing the revisionist viewpoint on the class line. It's pretty similar to the outlook of certain people today.

that nowadays relations between father and son would have become so intimate. What a wonderful form of "leftism" this is!

Enough of this! We're not going to waste any more ink in refuting this kind of stupid thinking. Let us do some investigation into the origin of this new type of racism!

This is nothing but the handiwork of revisionist elements. Why then should bourgeois elements want to oppress children of bourgeois origin? Isn't this odd? We think not. They do it precisely because these young people do not belong to the same class as themselves. As far as carrying out their restorationist scheme is concerned, they see no difference between children of proletarian origin and children of non-proletarian origin. Perhaps those young people who are hothouse flowers, who do not understand the world and who rest on their "natural redness" laurels are of more use to them. These schemers quickened their pace particularly after Chairman Mao's great call in 1962 to "never forget class struggle." In the situation of class struggle at that time, who did the spearhead point at? The major target was the powerholders within the Party taking the capitalist road and the snakes and monsters whom they sheltered. They perverted the idea stealthily in order to change the direction of the struggle. Originally, the father's *ch'eng-fen* ought to have been the son's origin, but now they've made the father's *ch'eng-fen* serve as the son's *ch'eng-fen*. Thus, under the guise of "class struggle," they have disregarded the Centre's directives and, by visible and invisible means, they have had a field day of large scale oppression. Youths of bad origin are their shield and oppression of these innate "criminals" has become their means of passing off dog meat for mutton, a gold-plated signboard which confuses people's senses! The Party Centre correctly pointed out that this was one of the sources of the line which was "left" in form but right in essence.

In carrying out this evil design, they made use of the force of old social customs, the naive innocence of young people and especially the blind arrogance of some children of high cadres (for example, they divided themselves into three categories since the terms "revolutionary armyman" and "revolutionary martyr" really meant the same as "revolutionary cadre" while the children of workers and peasants only qualified for categories four and five). They also made use of the defects and mistakes of a section of middle and lower-level cadres. Some cadres accepted and carried out this reactionary policy. This was an expression of theoretical ignorance, for they could not distinguish between Marxist-Leninist class theory and petty bourgeois only origin theory. In terms of their perspicacity, it shows how dim they were: they couldn't distinguish between young people's genuine [political] behaviour and their superficial behaviour. It showed their feeble workstyle: they couldn't give young people the opportunity to demonstrate their political thought through behaviour; they couldn't do political work. They used origin as a tool to further their work, to attack certain people and to encourage others. In political terms, it showed their declining enthusiasm: they didn't want to do careful investigations but were content to use origin as a slide rule. In terms of revolutionary consciousness, it showed their timidity: they didn't dare to promote people with genuinely good behaviour because they were afraid of the responsibility this entailed. Thus these factors combined to worsen the situation and created an absolutely intolerable phenomenon in our social system and alongside our Party. A new privileged stratum was created and, along with that, a new stratum suffering discrimination. However, this is a natural, unchangeable phenomenon. As Chairman Mao points out, racist oppression is in fact class oppression. These methods used by revisionist elements are also in fact the prelude to counter-revolutionary bourgeois restoration.[6] Nonetheless we must point out that the counter-revolutionary revisionist elements have obliterated the class line from the right since they are

---

6. When we were listing the crimes of the revisionist clique in victimising youths of bad origin, some people unexpectedly accused us of whitewashing the revisionist clique. That's not strange because they still think that oppressing youths of bad origin is a good thing. If someone were described as victimising "sons of bitches," then according to their bastard logic this amounts to a whitewash!

unscrupulously sheltering landlords, rich peasants, counter-revolutionaries, bad elements and rightists, since they are sheltering bourgeois elements. They brought gentlemanly bourgeois authorities into the Party, they gave certain five element people high salaries and talked a lot about peaceful coexistence with them. On the other hand, however, they victimised youths of bad origins, they victimised part of the successors to the revolutionary cause of the proletariat. If this isn't a bout of sharp and complex class struggle then what is it?

When the work teams were in control, they obliterated the class line by superficially extreme "left" methods. In dealing with the question of origin, they were really indistinguishable from the revisionist clique. As a result, not only was this serious social problem not solved, but its effect was deepened; the contradiction was made wider and more public. The brutal technique of "uprooting;" the so-called debate which was an insulting charade; the friskings, detentions, assaults and other such invasions of personal rights; the variety of methods they used to destroy the normal pattern of life of this section of young people; the motley measures they used to deprive them of their political rights. All this appeared under the guise of "transcending Mao Tse-tung Thought." This has caused so many people to become depressed, to feel like criminals without crimes, humiliated and ashamed. They could not devote all of their energy to the movement. They wanted to be revolutionary but they weren't allowed to have a stake in the revolution; they wanted to rebel but didn't meet the conditions for rebellion. This has sapped the enthusiasm of so many young people. It was this reactionary line which is responsible for reducing the revolutionary ranks. It has served the purposes of the reactionary line. Objectively speaking, it has served the purposes of sheltering the powerholders taking the capitalist road who had sneaked into the Party and of setting one part of the masses against another. There is good reason for raising this question. If this movement does not thoroughly liberate that large section of revolutionary youth who have been oppressed most grievously in the past, then it can in no way attain thorough victory!

Comrades, are we going to allow this kind of phenomena to continue? Should we not rise up and thoroughly clean up all this pollution? Should we not fill in the chasm created by these people? When the reactionaries were in power, not only were youths of bad origin oppressed, but also youths of worker-peasant origin and other revolutionary youths who opposed the clique in authority taking the capitalist road. We call on all those revolutionary youths who were victimised by the reactionaries to unite and organise under the banner of Mao Tse-tung Thought! Since you suffered the most deeply from bourgeois oppression, your opposition should be the most determined. When they are being criticised, you have the greatest right to speak. Mr T'an's group, who claimed falsely that they'd been victimised while in reality they'd been favoured, have no right to speak. If we rely on them to do the criticising, it cannot be deep and penetrating. You are not bystanders. You're masters of your own fate. Only cowards wait for others to hand things to them on a plate. Revolutionaries have always relied on struggle! You should defend Mao Tse-tung Thought and the Party's class line without shirking responsibility. Don't allow the revisionist clique to subvert it from the right nor the reactionary line to attack it from the "left." You should believe in your ability to carry out this glorious task victoriously! You should not reject youth who have not engaged in oppression and who are not prejudiced. You can unite with them and struggle and rise together. Comrades, we must believe in the Party and must remember Chairman Mao's teaching: "Real materialists know no fear!"

Victory will be ours!

All revolutionary youth who have suffered oppression, rise up and battle on courageously!

First draft: July 1966
Finished text: September 1966
Revised text: November 1966

SELECTED BIBLIOGRAPHY

Primary Sources

"Bring to light the inferior methods of the 'Peking Research Group on the Problem of Family Origin'," *Tung Feng Pao* [East Wind Report], March 19, 1967.

"The Central Committee of the CCP and the State Council decide to reform the methods of enrolment to higher level schools," *Kuang-ming Jih-pao* [Kuang-ming Daily], June 18, 1966.

Ch'en Yi, "Speech to students about to graduate from Peking's institutions of higher education," *Chung-kuo Ch'ing-nien* [China Youth], No.17, September 1, 1961, pp.2-5.

Ch'i Hsiang-tung, "Hail, line of the proletarian class!" printed by Ch'ih P'iao middle school of the Peking College for Petroleum Industry, trans. in *China News Analysis*, No. 636, November 11, 1966.

Ch'ien Chün-jui, "General Policy of Present Educational Construction," May 1950, in John N. Hawkins, trans., *Educational Theory in the People's Republic of China: The Report of Ch'ien Chün-jui*, Asian Studies at Hawaii, No.6, Asian Studies Program, University of Hawaii, 1971, pp.63-121.

"Decisions concerning the Differentiation of Class Status in the Countryside," adopted by the Government Administration Council for the Central People's Government on August 4, 1950, in *People's China* (supplement), Vol.II, No.8, October 16, 1950, pp.3-16.

Hsiang Nung, "The class policy which attaches importance to behaviour must be implemented," *Chung-kuo Ch'ing-nien* [China Youth], No.17, September 1, 1965, in *Selections from China Mainland Magazines* No.495, pp.35-38.

Liao Lu-yen, "Rural class status and land reform," *People's China* (supplement), Vol.II, No.8, October 16, 1950, pp.17-20.

Liu Shao-ch'i, "The Political Report of the Central Committee of the CPC to the Eighth National Congress of the Party," September 15, 1956, in *Eighth National Congress of the Communist Party of China* (Peking: Foreign Languages Press, 1956), Vol.I, pp.15-111.

"One ought to define and view correctly the family origin and class *ch'eng-fen* of youth and children," *Chung-kuo Ch'ing-nien* [China Youth], No.13, July 1, 1962, p.24.

"'Only origin theory' and 'origin theory' are both contrary to Marxism-Leninism and Mao Tse-tung Thought," *Tung Feng Pao* [East Wind Report], March 19, 1967.

"Origin Theory," by The Peking Research Group on the Problem of Family Origin, *Chung-hsüeh Wen-ko Pao* [Middle School Cultural Revolution News], special issue, February 1967.

"Sentence 'origin theory' to death," *Chiao-kung Chan-pao* [Educational Workers' Combat Bulletin], March 11, 1967.

"Stressing behaviour is the Party's class policy," *Chung-kuo Ch'ing-nien* [China Youth], No.18, September 16, 1965, pp.2-5.

Sun Yi-ch'ing, "Lay down the load; advance with light equipment," *Chung-kuo Ch'ing-nien Pao* [China Youth Daily], November 17, 1964, in *Survey of China Mainland Press* No.3349, pp.1-6.

Sun Yün-chieh, "I rebel against the exploiting class and join the Communist Party," *Chung-kuo Ch'ing-nien* [China Youth], No.16, August 16, 1965, pp.19-21.

Tsen-yang fen-hsi nung-ts'un chieh-chi [How to Analyse Rural Classes] (Peking: Jen-min Ch'u-pan-she, 1966).

Secondary Sources

Richard Baum, "'Red and Expert': The Politico-Ideological Foundations of China's Great Leap Forward," *Asian Survey*, September 1964, pp.1048-1057.

Gordon A. Bennett, "Political Labels and Popular Tension," *Current Scene*, February 26, 1969, pp.1-15.

Gordon A. Bennett and Ronald N. Montaperto, *Red Guard: The Political Biography of Dai Hsiao-ai* (New York, N.Y.: Anchor Books, 1972).

Jerome A. Cohen, *The Criminal Process in the People's Republic of China 1949-1963: An Introduction* (Cambridge, Mass.: Harvard University Press, 1968).

K.H. Fan, ed., *The Chinese Cultural Revolution: Selected Documents* (New York, N.Y.: Grove Press, 1968).

John Gardner, "Educated Youth and Urban-Rural Inequalities," in John W. Lewis, ed., *The City in Communist China* (Stanford, Calif.: Stanford University Press, 1971), pp.235-286.

William Hinton, "Hundred-Day War: The Cultural Revolution at Tsinghua University," *Monthly Review*, July-August 1972.

Richard Kraus, "The Evolving Concept of Class in Post-Liberation China" (Ph.D. Dissertation, Columbia University, 1974).

Ronald N. Montaperto, "From Revolutionary Successors to Revolutionaries: Chinese Students in the Early Stages of the Cultural Revolution," in Robert A. Scalapino, ed., *Elites in the People's Republic of China* (Seattle, Wash.: University of Washington Press, 1972), pp.575-605.

Donald J. Munro, "The Malleability of Man in Chinese Marxism," *The China Quarterly*, No.48, October-December 1971, pp.609-640.

Michel Oksenberg, "Occupational Groups in Chinese Society and the Cultural Revolution," in M. Oksenberg et al., *The Cultural Revolution: 1967 in Review*, Michigan Papers in Chinese Studies, No.2, 1968, pp.1-39.

Dennis Ray, "Red and Expert in China's Cultural Revolution," *Pacific Affairs*, Spring 1970, pp.22-33.

Dennis M. Ray, "Mao and the Classless Society," *Survey*, No.77, Autumn 1970, pp.30-50.

Robert Taylor, *Education and University Enrolment Policies in China, 1949-1971* (Canberra: Australian National University Press, 1973).

Martin K. Whyte, "'Red vs. Expert': Peking's Changing Policy," *Problems of Communism*, November-December 1972, pp.18-27.

Contemporary China Papers

The Contemporary China Centre was established in The Australian National University in 1970. It is an inter-disciplinary body, which gives cohesion to the studies of modern China carried out in various disciplines within the University. Its functions include co-ordination of research and co-operation with other Australian and overseas universities and with interested persons outside the academic world.

The work of the Centre involves three major Schools of the University: General Studies, Social Sciences and Pacific Studies. Each is represented on the Centre's Advisory Committee, of which Professor Wang Gungwu, Acting Director, Research School of Pacific Studies, is chairman and Miss Audrey Donnithorne and Dr Frederick C. Teiwes, from the same school, are, respectively, Head and Deputy Head.

Mainly the studies in the Contemporary China Papers, which will be the work of scholars at The Australian National University or visitors associated with its China program and of members of other Australian universities, will reflect the Centre's chief focus of interest: modern China and its foreign relations since 1949. They will also, however, include historical studies dealing with the pre-Communist period.

The aim of the series is to present some of the research being carried out in Australia on modern China, a subject of profound significance in international relations and one that stimulates lively interest and debate.

Information about future papers may be obtained from:
Contemporary China Papers
The Research School of Pacific Studies
P.O. Box 4
Canberra, A.C.T., Australia 2600